RAISING THE RIGOR

Effective **Questioning Strategies** *and* **Techniques** *for the Classroom*

Eileen Depka

Solution Tree | Press

a division of
Solution Tree

555 North Morton Street

Bloomington, IN 47404

800.733.6786 (toll free) / 812.336.7700

FAX: 812.336.7790

email: info@SolutionTree.com

SolutionTree.com

Visit **go.SolutionTree.com/instruction** to download the free reproducibles in this book.

Printed in the United States of America

21   20   19   18   17   2   3   4   5

Library of Congress Cataloging-in-Publication Data

Names: Depka, Eileen, author.

Title: Raising the rigor : effective questioning strategies and techniques

   for the classroom / Eileen Depka.

Description: Bloomington, IN : Solution Tree Press, 2017. | Includes

   bibliographical references and index.

Identifiers: LCCN 2016052043 | ISBN 9781942496984 (perfect bound)

Subjects: LCSH: Inquiry-based learning. | Interaction analysis in education.

   | Discussion. | Classroom management. | Effective teaching.

Classification: LCC LB1027.23 .D47 2017 | DDC 371.3/7--dc23 LC record available at https://lccn.loc.gov/2016052043

Solution Tree

Jeffrey C. Jones, CEO

Edmund M. Ackerman, President

Solution Tree Press

President and Publisher: Douglas M. Rife

Editorial Director: Sarah Payne-Mills

Managing Production Editor: Caroline Weiss

Senior Production Editor: Tonya Maddox Cupp

Senior Editor: Amy Rubenstein

Proofreader: Kendra Slayton

Text Designer and Compositor: Abigail Bowen

Cover Designer: Rian Anderson

Editorial Assistants: Jessi Finn and Kendra Slayton

ACKNOWLEDGMENTS

Thank you to the dedicated individuals at Solution Tree Press, who are clearly committed to providing quality resources to educators. A special thank you to Douglas Rife and Tonya Maddox Cupp for their support, guidance, and encouragement. It has been a privilege to work with an organization as impressive as Solution Tree.

Solution Tree Press would like to thank the following reviewers:

Melody Apezteguia
Mathematics Teacher
American Fork High School
American Fork, Utah

Lauren Brantley
Social Studies Teacher
Henderson Middle School
Atlanta, Georgia

Chelsea Collins
English Language Arts Teacher
Woodstown Middle School
Woodstown, New Jersey

Rick Joseph
5/6 Digital Literacy Workshop and Social
    Studies Teacher
Birmingham Covington School
Bloomfield Township, Michigan

Topher Kandik
English Language Arts Teacher
SEED PCS of Washington, DC
Washington, DC

Scott Slechta
English Language Arts Teacher
Fairfield High School
Fairfield, Iowa

Kimberly Thomas
Mathematics Teacher
Woodruff Career and Technical Center
Peoria, Illinois

Cathy Whitehead
Third-Grade Teacher
West Chester Elementary School
Henderson, Tennessee

Visit **go.SolutionTree.com/instruction** to download the free reproducibles in this book.

TABLE OF CONTENTS

Chapter 3

Developing Effective Assessments

Chapter 4

Ensuring Student Success With Complex Questions

Chapter 5

Creating Standards-Based Questions and Tasks

Chapter 6

Encouraging Traits to Attain College and Career Readiness

Chapter 7

Encouraging Student Involvement **83**

Chapter 8

Growing Students' Ability to Ask Questions That Matter . . . **95**

Epilogue

Pulling It All Together **103**

References and Resources **107**

Index **113**

ABOUT THE AUTHOR

Eileen Depka, PhD, has a background in assessment, common assessment design, rubric development, standards-based assessment, question design, classroom questioning practices, positive practices in grading and reporting, and the implementation of standards-based grading and reporting. She is the author of many books including *Bringing Homework Into Focus, Using Formative Assessment in the RTI Framework, Designing Rubrics for Mathematics, Designing Assessment for Mathematics,* and *The Data Guidebook for Teachers and Leaders.*

Eileen has supervised and coordinated curriculum, instruction, assessment, special education, educational technology, and continuous improvement efforts. She has taught all subjects at the elementary and middle school levels as well as graduate-level courses. She provides professional development for K–12 and undergraduate educators and, as a consultant, has worked across the country, focusing on creating engaging workshops tailored to meet a school's and district's individual needs.

She is passionate about student achievement and believes that all students can find academic success. Her goal is to work with teachers and administrators to collectively increase expertise and add to strategy banks used in schools to increase student performance.

Eileen earned a bachelor's degree in elementary and middle level education from the University of Wisconsin–Milwaukee, and she earned her master's and doctorate degrees from Cardinal Stritch University.

To book Eileen Depka for professional development, contact pd@SolutionTree.com.

INTRODUCTION

Teaching can bring us great joy and present huge challenges. It is rewarding and frustrating, often at the same time. It is a profession like no other. We can impact the lives of hundreds of young individuals. We can make a difference.

But teaching is a huge responsibility. Although we want what is best for our students, that path is not always clear. There are thrilling moments when students demonstrate their knowledge and skills successfully. There are moments of confusion when students state loudly and clearly, "We never learned this before!" regarding concepts that teachers covered the previous year. There is always need for a patient response, reteaching, reminders, and new experiences to solidify previous learning.

Some students engage in classroom discussion; others sit back and watch, probably still learning, but not through active involvement. Some students participate consistently, some occasionally, some not unless teachers invite them to respond. Some are confident in their ability to respond. Some are afraid. Some are simply disengaged. That's where this book comes in.

About This Book

This book provides information, strategies, and examples to use during classroom discussions as well as within assignments and assessments. It provides recommendations for effectively designing questions to set the stage for quality discussions that engage and inspire students. Promoting higher-order thinking skills not only actively engages students' minds but supports a deeper, more meaningful level of understanding. In the pages that follow, you will find easy and effective practices for accomplishing just that.

Chapter 1 lays the groundwork and highlights the impact that questioning techniques can have on student achievement. High-quality questions help students make connections among previously learned content and personal experiences. When questioning helps students discover, evaluate, and apply content, teachers have the opportunity to increase students' ability to analyze and use information to a greater extent. Students are more likely to experience success when applying their knowledge and skills to new or unique situations.

Chapter 2 concentrates on identifying, explaining, and providing examples for various questioning techniques and structures. This chapter also introduces the concept of higher-order thinking skills and takes a deep look at Bloom's (1956) taxonomy and its use for question development at a variety of sophistication levels. It shows you how Webb's (1997) Depth of Knowledge framework helps you align standards and tasks to levels of cognitive complexity. Visit **go.SolutionTree.com /instruction** for an interview with Dr. Norman Webb about the Depth of Knowledge.

In chapter 3, I discuss the connection between a question's intent and its format, including quality assessment practices and examples.

Chapter 4 provides examples of the types of support that students need to grow their ability to respond successfully to complex and rigorous questions. This section will consider the connection between complex questions, background knowledge, and text complexity. It highlights ways to scaffold questions and support student understanding. The strategies increase students' opportunities to succeed, because they're responding to questions designed with increased rigor and more sophisticated content.

A process in chapter 5 assists you in deconstructing standards' components so that you can develop quality questions based on those standards. It reveals connections between the types of questions generated and the level of complexity indicated within the standards. It provides templates and examples that will support the creation and organization of multiple standards-based questions. Standards-based assessments rely on questions generated through this process.

Chapter 6 delves into components related to questioning to support students in long-term success. It covers college and career readiness skills, including traits like critical thinking, perseverance, problem solving, and communication.

Laying groundwork that promotes an atmosphere of respect, collaboration, and openness to the ideas of others is the topic of chapter 7. It shares multiple techniques to institute questioning strategies that encourage advanced thought and discussion. Methods of evaluation show you how to analyze student beliefs and reflect on classroom practices.

Chapter 8 explains why students need to understand the art of questioning. I discuss practices that provide students with the ability to understand, respond to, and create questions at increased levels of sophistication. You will also find strategies for teaching students how to formulate questions that are at varied levels of difficulty.

The epilogue reiterates key points and provides a global summary of practices that promote a positive, productive approach to question design and implementation.

My goal is to give readers easy-to-implement strategies, templates, and examples to increase higher-order thinking skills and to deepen student understanding. Don't we all want students to think deeply?

CHAPTER 1

Using Questioning Strategies in the Classroom

There are only so many hours in a day. We have approximately 180 days in the classroom with students, and in an average day, a teacher is likely to spend about five solid hours with students. Clearly, our goal is to make the best use of that time. We want to use practices and strategies that will most benefit our students. We aim to use processes and procedures that increase our ability to get the most effective use from our time and that of our students.

And how do we determine effectiveness? Standards and content are the focus of education in the early 21st century. We use both to identify what is important for our students to learn. Evaluating student progress helps us evaluate those targets important to the lessons we teach and to better understand our students' performance levels. We evaluate data so that we can best meet all learners' needs. For example, the 2015 National Assessment of Educational Progress (NAEP) data show little progress and low student achievement (NAEP, n.d.). Reviewing and understanding these components, which we do in this chapter, helps us create a systematic approach to lesson identification and development.

If, as part of that approach, we take time to evaluate the types of questions we ask—even the ways we ask them—we will positively impact students' levels of understanding and performance. We can create different questioning strategies, as explained in this chapter. We even have the opportunity to develop habits in our students that will transcend the classroom. Our approach to formulating, posing, and responding to questions can increase students' curiosity, grow their problem-solving skills, escalate engagement levels, and strengthen their ability to persevere.

A Call to Action

Can we influence our students' academic abilities by being aware of the questions we ask and the way we ask them in the classroom? Evidence in the 2015 National Assessment of Educational Progress (NAEP, n.d.) definitely shows a need for a boost in U.S. academic performance. The NAEP is a U.S. standardized test that evaluates and reports student progress in a variety of subjects including mathematics and reading. The assessment compares subject-level achievement across states.

The 2015 NAEP results reveal that 40 percent of fourth-grade students are proficient or higher in mathematics. In eighth grade, that number is 33 percent. Reading results show proficiency levels of 36 percent and 34 percent in fourth and eighth grades, respectively. It's not because teachers aren't dedicated to boosting academic performance but because those devoted teachers keep searching for strategies that will positively impact student performance. Figure 1.1 shows NAEP results in mathematics, and figure 1.2 shows NAEP results in reading, illustrating how U.S. students have fared over time. The results in both subjects show little variation since 2005.

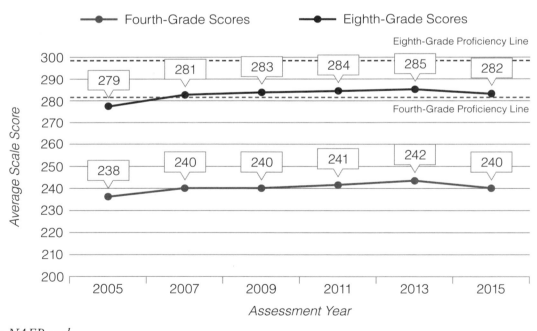

Source: NAEP, n.d.

Figure 1.1: NAEP results in mathematics over time.

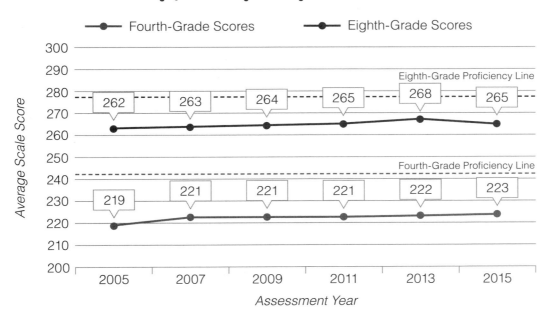

Source: NAEP, n.d.

Figure 1.2: NAEP results in reading over time.

Reviewing the figures shows us that in mathematics and in reading, in fourth grade and in eighth grade, the average national scale scores are well below the established proficiency level. The dotted lines on each chart indicate the proficiency level for each grade level.

If NAEP results are an accurate illustration of the performance level of students in the United States, it seems the data strongly suggest that a call to action is in order. With the highest level of performance at 40 percent, the results are not something that we would be proud of in our own classrooms. Growing these scores to reach or at least be near proficiency requires a change. Although making a significant change in these scores may seem like an insurmountable task, change happens one classroom at a time. Tests results like the Programme for International Student Assessment (PISA) can determine strengths and challenges by subject and country. Fifteen-year-olds take tests in mathematics, science, and reading. In 2012, about 28 million students took the PISA (Organisation for Economic Co-operation and Development, n.d.). Results, at www.oecd.org/pisa/keyfindings/pisa-2012-results.htm, can be compared. No matter what the assessment, the goal is to learn from the data and act to support student learning.

Teachers care about their students. They put a lot of effort into planning and presenting lessons designed to help students succeed. What do we do when results reflect that less than half, in most cases only a third, of students are proficient? More important, can the questions we ask in the classroom better prepare students to successfully apply knowledge and skills to tasks on standardized tests?

In short: yes. Reviewing multiple sample problems from the NAEP shows that students apply their knowledge and skills to questions. If we equip students to respond primarily to questions that require recall or performance of common tasks, we are certainly providing them with important foundational skills. However, if the level of sophistication stops there, students will not acquire the skills necessary to perform at increased levels of success—not only on standardized tests but in real-life experiences.

My intention is not to highlight increased standardized test performance as our end goal but to concentrate on how the questions teachers use within our classrooms can have a positive impact on student success within and beyond school walls. Standardized tests provide measures of performance and inform schools of their status in comparison to others. However, the purpose of academic measures is to use the information to increase student understanding. Increased understanding will likely result in enhanced performance on standardized tests, but the end goal is to help students achieve higher levels of success. Increased test scores are a byproduct. Interestingly, even though many teachers realize the benefits of infusing higher-order thinking skills into classroom experiences, practices are heavily weighted toward recall questions. Some have noted that since the 1950s, classroom practices associated with questioning types and techniques have changed little (Fisher & Frey, 2007). However, teachers who are trained in ways of creating and implementing a variety of questions are more likely to use them (King, Goodson, & Rohani, n.d.). When the classroom questions asked go beyond recall and provide students with opportunities to think critically, students will have experiences that lead to higher levels of expertise.

Making a Difference With Questioning Strategies

Questioning methods have been studied for centuries. The ancient Greek philosopher Socrates was known for his ability to pose questions in order to generate meaningful discussions.

More recently, however, John Dewey promoted the importance of deep questioning in his 1910 title, *How We Think*. Dewey (1910) refers to thinking as a state of doubt leading to investigations that prove or nullify one's beliefs. In addition, thinking helps us discover the meaning and importance of subject matter. Dewey explains that limiting thought to memorization or recall is contrary to creating an atmosphere where the mind is trained to think and process. He therefore promotes questions that challenge the mind and create situations where thinking occurs at deep and complex levels.

Within the methods we use to generate the questions we ask, there is room for change, perhaps even growth. If we find ways to increase student engagement, students will learn more and perhaps perform at higher levels. According to Robyn Jackson and Allison Zmuda (2014), students can be compliant without being engaged. Engagement requires that students be involved in complex thinking.

Many students find straightforward, lower-level questions boring; richer questions are intellectually stimulating, and students find them engaging. Lower-level questions might include specific dates, names, and places. These questions might have value in certain contexts but should go beyond the factual. Richer questions can include those that compare and contrast events or explain why a date is important historically and how the events impacted future events. To support higher-order thinking skills, teachers need to pose questions to students they have not been asked before. Even complex questions can be a recall experience if a student answered previously. When we create an atmosphere in which students experience acceptable challenge, they achieve success. Increasing engagement, interest, and motivation in the classroom—regardless of their current levels—are certainly appealing ventures. Students become motivated to learn because learning matters to them. What we ask and the way we pose questions do impact our students. The way we challenge our students through the questions we ask can create personal meaning and associations with previously learned content—all of which leads to a new level of understanding (Cushman, 2014).

Consider other reasons to change things up in the classroom by increasing the variety of questions you present. In her *Phi Delta Kappan* article "Neuroscience Reveals that Boredom Hurts," Judy Willis (2014) asserts that the student brain wants stimulation and the lack thereof results in boredom, which hinders productivity. Repetitious tasks and simplistic questioning lead to apathy and decreased levels of performance. Student interest is piqued—and a net positive result achieved—when stimulating discussion is inspired by interesting and engaging questions.

Those questions don't just benefit students; they benefit teachers as well. But getting to strong questioning strategies takes perseverance. Expect a transitional time. Applying a process to questions will make for purposeful questions. The following sections explain these topics.

Benefitting Both Students and Teachers

Students are not the only ones who benefit from varied and higher levels of questions. Teachers can focus student thinking on those learning targets that matter most. Responses provide insights into students' levels of understanding, which then become tools for increasing student awareness (Clough, 2007).

The processes, activities, and lessons we use to help students discover, evaluate, and apply content give teachers the opportunity to increase students' ability to analyze and use information. We can design questions to help students think, process, and internalize information. Investigating responses to interesting and engaging questions strengthens knowledge and skills (Walsh & Sattes, 2005).

Charlotte Danielson (2007) recognizes questioning and discussion techniques as important components of effective teaching. Danielson, a well-established reference for teacher evaluation, asks that questioning techniques specifically enhance student learning. A function of classroom query is to provide the class with multiple opportunities to respond to open-ended questions. Encouraging divergent thinking helps students to make connections and deepen their understanding of a topic.

Danielson (2007) further supports increasing the ability of students to ask questions. In her vision, students dialogue around meaningful questions while the teacher facilitates the discussion, but students carry the weight of the content and conversation. Students answer questions so teachers can check their understanding, and questions allow them to deepen their understanding. Quality questioning strategies result in an intellectually active classroom that gives students the opportunity to engage at heightened levels of sophistication, intensified awareness, and increased comprehension.

Requiring Transition and Perseverance

As we strive to increase the complexity associated with what we ask our students, the change in practice may be a challenge for our students. Their experience might be one of questions that require them to recall information or repeatedly perform a procedure. Questions that require memorization or one-word answers might be their norm. "What does a plant need to grow?" "What is the answer to the mathematics problem?" "What world leaders played a key role in World War I?" While transitioning from a more familiar approach to one that requires additional challenge, students are likely to need support to go beyond their comfort zone. A byproduct of the transition could be an increase in initial failures. If educators and students view failure as a step closer to success, the change will be more palatable. I often tell students that they are on the road to right. They may not experience the highest level of success initially, but they are on the way. Teachers need to create a balance of challenge and support in order for students to be willing to engage (Quate & McDermott, 2014).

In her book *Mindset*, Carol Dweck (2006) identifies perseverance as another benefit of a system of questioning that promotes deep thought, which supports the long-term success of our students. According to Dweck (2006), we as a society formerly believed those who had to spend more time learning were struggling learners. She reveals that even the highly gifted work hard in order to achieve. Students who typically learn quickly without struggle need to spend time and effort to find appropriate responses to questions that challenge them. Accomplishment is closely tied to effort regardless of individual or perceived ability. This reminds me of the famous Thomas Edison quote regarding his development of the light bulb. He said, "I have not failed ten thousand times . . . I have succeeded in proving that those ten thousand ways will not work" (Edison as quoted in Furr, 2011). If we encourage our students to think and try—and when they fail, to think and try some more—we will take them to a place of deeper understanding, greater success, and a heightened level of perseverance. It is through their willingness to persevere that they'll realize success. We can challenge our students to think just beyond their comfort level and provide support as they experience roadblocks so they can move toward perseverance through a gradual release approach. Teachers can help grow perseverance by working with students on challenging activities then weaning that support as students begin persevering on their own. Scaffold activities to provide the stepping stones necessary to lead to higher levels of challenge. Provide the resources or locations of resources needed for students to be successful. Ask questions that will lead students to successful outcomes rather than provide answers for them. See the teacher do it in the following example.

Teacher: *Students, throughout the year we will be involved in various tasks that require us to give increased amounts of effort. Sometimes things come easy for us. Think of a time when you had to try something more than once to be successful at it. Who has an idea to share?*

Student: *I had trouble learning to ride a bike. It took lots of time and practice before I could ride and not fall.*

Teacher: *I would imagine that many of us had a similar experience. We didn't give up, though. Even though it was difficult for us, we kept trying. We were motivated to be on the bike, and to be able to ride successfully. Why do you think you continued to try and you didn't give up?*

Student: *Because I wanted to get places faster, and I wanted to ride with my friends.*

Teacher: *This type of effort is called perseverance. Perseverance means that even when something is difficult for us, we keep trying. In order to become good at using the knowledge and skills we gain in school, we need to persevere in the classroom just like we do when learning a new skill at home, like riding a bike. We learn things in school so that we can become successful at applying our abilities to tasks that are like those found in the real world.*

For example, this week in mathematics we learned to find the area and perimeter of various shapes. Today we are going to use that skill in a real-life situation. It will take multiple steps to arrive at a solution. You will need to determine how you will find your final answer and carry out a plan to do so. It will take perseverance.

Applying a Process

Using a process or cycle, explained in chapter 5 (page 63), to identify questions supports a purposeful approach to developing questions for the classroom (Fusco, 2012). These processes focus all questions on the goals of the lesson by planning the core questions in advance. *How* will you present the questions and acknowledge them? That is another point of planning. An atmosphere of respect and openness that builds levels of trust in the classroom supports the process.

Chapter 7 (page 83) explains how to create that culture. Process options and crucial components appear in chapter 4 (page 51).

Without applying careful thought to planning and posing questions, the result can be ineffective. An approach that includes preplanning questions to ensure addressed standards and content will bring a positive result. Preplanning questions help provide a balance that ensures higher-order thinking questions. Follow questions designed to solicit responses that prove students have the factual understanding needed with questions that inspire thought. For example, during a science unit on weather, younger students will learn a bit about temperature and seasons, but they also need to understand how weather impacts them, what they wear, and the activities they might be able to engage in outside. Preplanning questions cause a systematic approach to accomplishing the lesson's goals. They reveal confidence that students will reach the level of understanding required to succeed with lesson content. One way to make certain that questions promote in-depth critical thinking is to use a structure to level questions, using a taxonomy. Structures associated with classroom practice also support positive, productive, and engaging classroom conversations (Fisher & Frey, 2007).

In Summary

Student success is our end goal, not only for the short time students are with us but in their postschool lives. We want students to think, learn, and grow. That learning may appear in classroom performance, standardized assessments, or postsecondary success. Asking rich questions in the classroom will encourage thought and promote understanding. We support perseverance, engagement, and communication skills through the use of high-quality questioning strategies. Forethought and preplanning questions provide a foundation that supports effective teaching.

CHAPTER 2
Deconstructing Higher-Order Thinking Skills

Higher-order thinking skills can set the stage for more detailed conversations about questioning strategies. Higher-order thinking skills enable students to apply knowledge and skills in a variety of unique situations. Students are engaged in processes often requiring real-world applications. Tasks teachers develop to support these skills often have multiple solutions and multiple paths to correct solutions. To fully engage in situations that require this level of interaction with content, students need foundational background information (King, Goodson, & Rohani, n.d.). As teachers introduce content, they should consider the response to three questions: (1) What background knowledge and vocabulary are necessary for students to better understand the next unit? (2) Can connections be made with what is about to be learned to what students already know? and (3) What real-world connections can be made to relate the content and concepts to their purpose and importance outside of school? As content is introduced, regularly incorporate responses to these three questions. Chapter 4 discusses background knowledge in more detail.

Building a foundation for students can require the use of lower-order skills like recall, as is explained in Webb's Depth of Knowledge (DOK) framework (Webb, 1997, 1999). The key is to not stop there. When students demonstrate comprehension, they need to move beyond and be given ample opportunity to demonstrate understanding using methods unfamiliar to them. Application of higher-order thinking skills requires instruction, practice, and repetition. Multiple opportunities to employ these skills support and extend the ability of students to experience success (Brookhart, 2014).

You can design tasks that build these skills. This chapter offers Bloom's taxonomy and Webb's Depth of Knowledge, which help you promote higher-order thinking through task design, followed by a template to help you formulate those tasks. How will you know students are engaged in higher-order thinking when they tackle those tasks? This chapter tells you the indicators to look for. Bloom's taxonomy provides a structure with which to evaluate the sophistication of the work students are being asked to perform. Webb's Depth of Knowledge assists in understanding the cognitive complexity of the standards and the task intended to measure the standards.

Building Higher-Order Thinking Skills With Tasks

Meaningful tasks promote higher levels of thinking. Authentic, performance-based assessments provide a structure for students to intellectually engage with the content. These tasks characteristically:

- Involve the learner's skills, imagination, and originality
- Require students to use skills that will prepare them for life
- Remain rooted in realism
- Have a clear purpose that extends beyond the classroom
- Increase cognitive engagement

Good tasks are most often associated with real-world problems, which help students associate classroom skills with their purpose in life. Students recognize that they can transfer skills to uses beyond the classroom, and that gives them a purpose beyond a request of the teacher (Burke, 2009). For example, at some point in mathematics, students learn to use formulas to find the areas of a square, rectangle, and triangle. A task provides real-world experience if students have to find the area of a nontraditional shape—the area of an oddly shaped room, or a spot on the playground or parking lot, for example. This requires students to use their knowledge of area and apply it to the real world, applying formulas they know to solve an unknown.

When developing a higher-order thinking skills task, consider the following steps.

1. Identify the standards and content to address.

2. Determine ways in which the standards and content are applicable to a real-world situation.

3. Create a scenario that will engage the students in a task that requires them to apply their knowledge and skills to a new and unique situation. One effective way to create the task is to determine a situation in which students can apply the skills, state the situation, and create the need for student involvement. Flexibility in the methods that students use to complete the task will provide more opportunity for the use of higher-order thinking skills.

4. Determine the task requirements. Specifically, decide what students need to accomplish in order to successfully complete the task.

5. Identify the task evaluation criteria and the tool. Establish the characteristics that should be evident within a successful performance.

The following section provides a template that facilitates task design.

Using a Template to Design Tasks

The template in figure 2.1 can assist when you are designing tasks. Template completion requires the following information.

- Standards and Content: In this portion of the template, list the specific standards and content on which the task will focus. After creating the task, revisit this section to ensure that it measures the standards and content it intended to measure.

- Task Scenario: Design a task scenario that places the student into a real-life situation that they will need to solve. The task should indicate the problem and the required outcome. Avoid telling students what they will do. Let students determine the best path to obtain a solution.

- Task Requirements: Provide a list of any expectations connected to the task solution. This would include any specifics as to the format of the solution, components to be included in the response, and any supporting information that might be necessary.

- Evaluation Method: Share a rubric, point scale, or any other method of evaluation. Provide criteria for success to students prior to completing the task.

Subject:	
Unit of Study:	
Standards and Content	
Task Scenario	
Task Requirements	
Evaluation Method	

Figure 2.1: Developing higher-order thinking skills tasks.

*Visit **go.SolutionTree.com/instruction** for a free reproducible version of this figure.*

The templates can be used across subjects and curricula. Figure 2.2 provides an example of English language arts study with a completed template.

Subject: *English language arts*	
Unit of Study: *Research*	
Standards and Content	*Draw evidence from literary or informational texts to support analysis, reflection, and research.*
Task Scenario	*The school counselors are developing a class to help teenagers be successful and have a positive image of themselves and their lives. As they brainstormed the topics they want to include, they wondered if television commercials have an influence on teenagers. They have requested our help. You are being asked to determine the impact of TV commercials on the self-image of teenagers.*
Task Requirements	*Things to include:* • *Research studies and findings on the topic* • *Examples* • *Summary of evidence* • *Your conclusions based on your evidence* *Finished project:* • *Presentation in the format of your choice highlighting your work and conclusions*
Evaluation Method	*Rubric*

Source for Standard: National Governors Association Center for Best Practices (NGA) & Council of Chief State School Officers (CCSSO), 2010a.

Figure 2.2: Template for English language arts skills.

Figure 2.3 provides an example of a class some schools might call a *special* with art as the subject.

Subject: *Art*	
Unit of Study: *Two-dimensional drawing*	
Standards and Content	• *Know the elements and principles of design.* • *Understand what makes quality design.* • *Use design techniques to improve or change artwork.* • *Develop the craft and skills to produce quality art.*

Task Scenario	The Anderson Paper Company is looking for a new way to advertise their paper bags. In the past, they have told consumers how the bags can be used, but they feel people already know that. They want to start a campaign that shows their bags in an interesting and beautiful way. They've asked that you crush, twist, and crease their paper bags to create a display exhibiting the bags in unique forms.
Task Requirements	Using charcoal or pencils, create a two-dimensional copy of the image that can appear in their ad campaign.
Evaluation Method	Rubric

Figure 2.3: Template for art skills.

The template works not just for arts and humanities, but for sciences as well. Figure 2.4 is a completed template for a science-related task.

Subject: Science	
Unit of Study: Weather	
Standards and Content	Collect information and answer questions related to scientific questions. Use evidence to support explanations or solutions.
Task Scenario	Your family is considering moving to a different city. Their choices are Miami, Florida; Buffalo, New York; and Tucson, Arizona. They would like to consider weather as a factor in their decision-making process and are asking for your help. Research the weather in the three cities and provide your family with information to make their decision.
Task Requirements	Include precipitation and temperature through all months of the year. Research weather events that have impacted the locations. Determine other aspects of weather important to include in your research. Create ways to organize and compare the information you compile. Highlight the impact of weather in each location, stating the benefits and difficulties for each location.
Evaluation Method	Rubric

Figure 2.4: Template for science skills.

Design tasks to fit within a shorter or more extended time frame depending on the complexity of the task. If less time is available, construct a task that relates to the same standards but is more simplistic in nature. You can simplify tasks by limiting the expectations and by supplying tools or organizational structures to complete the task. For example, figure 2.5 shares a task to demonstrate knowledge and application of area and perimeter. You can alter the task for simplicity and time constraints by:

- Using a room in the school instead of a room outside of school

- Supplying the tools students need to measure the room

- Incorporating teamwork

- Sharing catalogs or advertisements so students can determine pricing

- Providing charts to facilitate students' organization of findings

Subject: *Mathematics*	
Unit of Study: *Area and Perimeter*	
Standards and Content	*Solve real-world and mathematical problems involving perimeters of polygons.*
Task Scenario	*The carpeting and the floor molding in your bedroom are going to be replaced. You have been asked to determine how much of each product is needed and to calculate the approximate cost.*
Task Requirements	*Find the area and perimeter of your room. Using resources available to you, find the cost of your choice of carpeting and molding. Determine the unit cost and full cost of each. Organize your information in an easy-to-understand document.*
Evaluation Method	*Rubric*

Source for standard: NGA & CCSSO, 2010b.

Figure 2.5: Template for mathematics skills.

Indicators of Student Engagement in Higher-Order Thinking Skills

Students who are processing information at higher levels show certain characteristics. Being aware of these attributes can help us evaluate student qualities and provide individual support needed to grow the characteristics. The criteria can help measure the growth in students' levels of comfort and ability as they become more familiar with higher-order thinking (Brookhart, 2010; Copeland, 2005).

The indicators of success include the following.

- Increased willingness to persevere in solving problems or completing tasks
- The ability to see a problem from a variety of perspectives
- The identification of more than one solution to a task
- Insight into multiple methods to arrive at a solution
- The ability to support solutions with evidence
- Increased ability to clearly communicate solutions
- Willingness to collaborate and listen to the perspectives of others
- The ability to create and follow a plan of action
- The ability to scrutinize, select, and use information that positively assists in completing the task
- The ability to organize conclusions and evidence into charts, graphs, visual displays, or other methods so that the outcome can be interpreted and understood by others

Clear communication, though not necessarily an indicator of success, is a byproduct. Monitor communication growth as well with the criteria checklist (figure 2.6). It identifies the current status of students regarding higher-order thinking skills and provides a framework for measuring their progress. Share the assessment criteria with students so they are aware of the indicators of success. When a teacher stresses the criteria, students make the connection between their own skill development and their ability to successfully engage in higher-order thinking tasks. Use the criteria to evaluate performance and growth throughout the year. Figure 2.6 provides space to evaluate each criterion on three separate dates.

Student name:	Date:				Date:				Date:			
Criteria:	1	2	3	4	1	2	3	4	1	2	3	4
Student shows perseverance when problem solving.												
Student sees the problems from various perspectives.												
Student identifies multiple ways to solve problems or complete tasks.												

Figure 2.6: Higher-order thinking skills criteria checklist.

continued →

*Visit **go.SolutionTree.com/instruction** for a free reproducible version of this figure.*

Criteria												
Student supports thinking with evidence.												
Student clearly communicates thinking.												
Student collaborates well with others.												
Student listens to the perspectives of others.												
Student develops and follows a plan to find a solution.												
Student identifies information important to the task solution.												
Student organizes information successfully.												
Student clearly communicates solutions.												

1 = No evidence of criterion 2 = Occasionally shows evidence 3 = Often shows evidence
4 = Regularly demonstrates criterion

When using the higher-order thinking skills criteria checklist, fill in all squares when students achieve a proficiency level. Doing so creates a visual representation that is easy to interpret. In other words, fill in Levels 1, 2, 3, and 4 if a student is at a Level 4. Figure 2.7 provides an example. A student consistently receiving a 1 in "identifies information important to the task solution" requires help distinguishing between the crucial and the superficial. Without support, the student will continue struggling with other components. The shaded squares could show growth, strengths, or challenge areas depending on the number and pattern created as squares are filled in. You can share the chart with students to set growth goals. Students can also benefit from completing a self-rating and comparing it with the teacher's observations.

Student name:	Date: Sep 20				Date: Oct 20				Date: Nov 20			
Criteria:	1	2	3	4	1	2	3	4	1	2	3	4
Student shows perseverance when problem solving.	■				■	■			■	■	■	
Student sees the problems from various perspectives.	■	■			■				■	■	■	■
Student identifies multiple ways to solve problems or complete tasks.	■				■				■			
Student supports thinking with evidence.	■				■				■			
Student clearly communicates thinking.	■				■				■			
Student collaborates well with others.	■				■				■		■	
Student listens to the perspectives of others.	■				■				■			
Student develops and follows a plan to find a solution.					■				■			

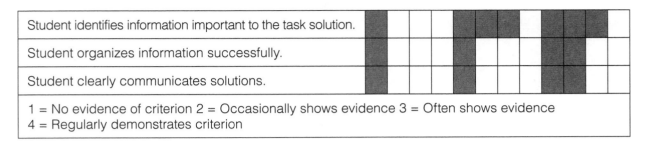

Student identifies information important to the task solution.								
Student organizes information successfully.								
Student clearly communicates solutions.								

1 = No evidence of criterion 2 = Occasionally shows evidence 3 = Often shows evidence
4 = Regularly demonstrates criterion

Figure 2.7: Higher-order thinking skills criteria checklist—sample.

To keep track of all students on a single page, tweak the format slightly. You can set up the chart similar to a traditional gradebook. Figure 2.8 (page 22) illustrates an alternative view. To record results, place the appropriate proficiency level in each cell at each administration. To enhance the view, color code the cells to create an easily interpreted visual display (1 = red, 2 = yellow, 3 = green, and 4 = blue). Although this format could be more convenient, it would be more difficult to use as a visual when conferencing with individuals about their progress (because multiple students appear on the same grid).

Recording students' progress based on specified criteria is a great start to measuring growth, but that alone will not ensure that skills increase. Teaching students the criteria for success expedites the ability to successfully demonstrate the characteristics.

A first step in growing student capacity is to share the indicators with students, then concentrate on each criterion, one at a time. That will make criteria clear to them. For example, you might give the following introduction to introduce perspective.

Teacher: *Students, throughout the year we will be involved in analyzing situations that require a look from different perspectives. Can you think of a time when you looked at a situation differently than someone else? Perhaps you both saw the situation accurately, but your perspectives were very different?*

Student: *I am in one now. I want to get my driver's license because not only do most of my friends have one, but I want to be less dependent on other people. That's my perspective. My mom is worried that something will happen to me if I drive, so she wants me to wait. My dad is fine with me getting one but doesn't know if he has the time to help me practice driving. My little brother can't wait because he wants me to take him to his baseball practices. That's four different perspectives on just one thing in my life.*

Teacher: *I would imagine that many of us have had a similar experience, maybe on the same or different topics. Understanding the perspectives of those involved in a situation can help us better understand the situation, responses to the situation, and possible solutions.*

Student Names:	Student shows perseverance when problem solving.		Student sees the problems from various perspectives.		Student identifies multiple ways to solve problems or complete tasks.		Student supports thinking with evidence.		Student clearly communicates thinking.	
	Dates:		Dates:		Dates:		Dates:		Dates:	

Student collaborates well with others.		Student listens to the perspectives of others.		Student develops and follows a plan to find a solution.		Student identifies information important to the task solution.		Student organizes information successfully.		Student clearly communicates solutions.	
Dates:		Dates:		Dates:		Dates:		Dates:		Dates:	

Figure 2.8: Higher-order thinking skills criteria checklist—multiple students.

Visit *go.SolutionTree.com/instruction* for a free reproducible version of this figure.

Student: It does help understanding what others are thinking. It makes it easier to know how to approach the situation or respond to their comments or actions.

Teacher: Understanding perspectives will promote understanding of the historical events that we will discuss throughout the year. We can evaluate cause and effect, but without analyzing the perspectives of those involved, we may never truly understand why an event happened in the first place and why it is historically important.

This is not a one-time conversation but one that should be revisited throughout the year. Teachers and students can continue to provide examples of perseverance both inside and outside the classroom. Students can track their growth in the skill when reflecting on their performance using the higher-order thinking skills criteria checklist highlighted in figure 2.6 (page 19).

A conversation about perseverance might also be appropriate prior to a state or standardized testing experience. Students can be reminded that, in order to successfully apply their knowledge and skills, some situations command a greater level of perseverance. When the path to a solution is not immediately recognizable, we don't give up. Instead, we read the problem again and again until a plan of attack surfaces. Perseverance is a characteristic that can be learned and developed.

Table 2.1 (page 24) lists some of the benefits of engaging in the use of higher-order thinking skills. Checking for engagement sometimes looks like directly asking students what they think. The ultimate goal is to help students understand the connection between the questions they encounter and the skill development they experience. Secondly, we want them to be able to understand that the skills are beneficial to them beyond school. The conversation points in the right column of table 2.1 should help students make connections between the skill and how it is currently beneficial to themselves and others. The questions that students ask and answer have the potential of helping them achieve the benefits and skills discussed in the left column, including increased perseverance and collaboration. The conversation points in the right column help students realize the importance of the benefits associated with skill development enhanced through responding to complex questions. Either students or teachers can ask those questions.

Students grow in their ability to interact with content when they are engaged in tasks and projects that promote higher-order thinking skills. Although projects are not necessarily related to a specific type of question or questioning technique, they serve to broaden the experiences of students and place them in situations that expand their horizons. Paying attention to the indicators associated with successful application of higher-order thinking skills can help monitor current status and growth. Teach the skills in the checklist so that students can achieve greater success in their ability to use higher-order thinking skills. As students grow in perseverance and use skills known to promote higher-order thinking, they will be more comfortable responding to questions that challenge and take them out of their comfort zone.

Table 2.1: Establishing Purpose With Students—Develop Questioning Expertise

The skills identified support a productive and successful life. Use the conversation points to help students recognize and appreciate the value.

Potential Impact Associated With Higher-Order Thinking Skills	Conversation Points
Increase perseverance, our ability to stick with something that is difficult for us.	Share a time when something was difficult for you, but you stuck with it. What was the result? (Examples: playing an instrument, participating in a sport)
Look at a problem from different points of view. If we can see multiple sides of a problem, we are more likely to find one or more solutions.	Share a time when you and a friend saw things differently. What was the result? What is the benefit to having different points of view?
Identify multiple ways to solve a problem. When there are multiple solutions, we have choices and can use what works best for us.	When you have a problem, why might it be good to have a variety of ways to solve it?
Understand the importance of supplying evidence. We are more likely to get our point across or be taken seriously when there is evidence to support what we say.	How do you think evidence might support your opinion when wanting to convince a parent to get you something you want?
Strengthen our ability to communicate our thoughts. Others will find it easier to understand us.	Can you describe a situation when you either had trouble getting your idea across or were with someone who was having trouble explaining his or her thoughts?
Learn collaboration skills. This increases our ability to successfully work with different types of people.	How do you think the ability to work with others effectively is important to you now and in your future?
Increase our ability to listen to perspectives. When we become better at listening, we are more likely to understand others.	How can actively listening to others benefit you in or outside of school?
Increase our skills at organizing information. When we are better at organizing information, it is easier for us to interpret and use.	Describe something that you have organized. Why did you organize it, and how has that helped you? (Example: A baseball card collection)
Identify information important to the task solution. When we can tell the difference between what is important and what is not, it is likely that the solution will achieve a positive result.	Describe a situation where it might be helpful to distinguish between important and less important information. (Example: Witnessing an event and telling someone about it)
Increase our ability to develop and follow a plan to find a solution. A plan gives us a roadmap to a potential solution. Without a plan we may or may not achieve a successful end.	Share a situation in which you think a plan is important to experience success. (Example: Going on a vacation)

Connecting Bloom's Taxonomy to Higher-Order Thinking Skills

A *taxonomy* is a classification system that provides order to a broader category or field. Benjamin Bloom and colleagues developed a taxonomy in 1956 as a way to promote the exchange of test items between universities. The intent was to classify the items into like educational objectives (Krathwohl, 2002). Bloom's taxonomy is a tool you can use to promote higher-order thinking skills in students.

Introduction and Terminology

The original taxonomy had six major categories on a continuum from simple to complex: (1) knowledge, (2) comprehension, (3) application, (4) analysis, (5) synthesis, and (6) evaluation. One intention of the framework was to help educators understand how people acquire new knowledge. The original taxonomy was intended to be a hierarchical system with students starting at the least complex end of the system and working their way up through the framework. It is often represented as a pyramid similar to the illustration in figure 2.9. Use of the taxonomy grew over time especially within education. Among other places, undergraduate programs used it for teaching students.

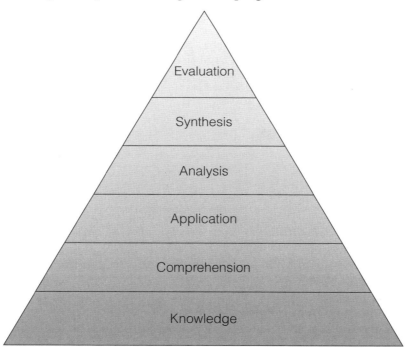

Figure 2.9: Original Bloom's taxonomy—pyramid format.

In 2001, Lorin Anderson and his former colleague David Krathwohl led a team that revised the taxonomy (Anderson & Krathwohl, 2001). The revision changed the framework from a list of nouns to a two-dimensional approach separating a knowledge dimension from the cognitive-process dimension. The cognitive-process dimension includes the categories of remember, understand, apply, analyze, evaluate, and create. The knowledge dimension includes factual, conceptual, procedural, and metacognitive knowledge (Krathwohl, 2002).

Figure 2.10 is a comparison between the original and revised versions of Bloom's taxonomy. The original version contains nouns while the revised version concentrates on actions. One shift in the organization connects to the hierarchy, which the figure also shows. *Evaluation* now appears in the second-highest position in the taxonomy. The word *create* replaced the word *synthesis* and was placed at the top of the list. The diagram has been moved out of the popular triangle format so that it doesn't appear as though more emphasis or time should be spent on the more simplistic verbs at the base of the triangle. Although the verbs appear according to their level of sophistication, we don't need to view it as a step-by-step hierarchy. When using the taxonomy as a tool to provide guidance in the creation of classroom questions, we can start at the level that best fits our purpose.

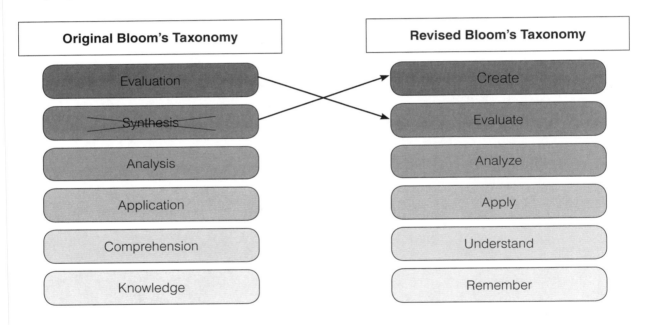

Figure 2.10: Comparison of the original and revised versions of Bloom's taxonomy.

A matrix can represent two domains so one can consider the intersection of the domain aspects when planning lessons or assessments. Table 2.2 provides an example of the type of activity that could coincide within each intersection.

Bloom's Taxonomy in Action

Bloom's taxonomy is a tool to create questions that drive students to higher levels of thought while scaffolding the information based on student needs. Developing the questions that teachers will use as part of instruction and assessment is an important part of the lesson- or unit-planning process. The following three steps provide an approach to identifying questions based on Bloom's taxonomy.

Table 2.2: Bloom's Taxonomy Dimensions

	Remember (Access knowledge from memory.)	Understand (Make meaning of information.)	Apply (Use information in various situations.)	Analyze (Relate parts to the whole; break apart information to investigate.)	Evaluate (Make judgments based on evidence.)	Create (Produce something original or recreate something known.)
Factual (Knowledge of terms, details, settings)	Write the names of states on a blank map of the United States.	Summarize an article in one's own words.	Follow a mathematical procedure to arrive at a solution.	Place topics or ideas into categories.	Provide critical feedback on a presentation.	Create a story based in a specific historical setting.
Conceptual (Knowledge of interrelationships of ideas, theories, principles)	Identify the differences between the original and new versions of Bloom's taxonomy.	Describe the relationships between weather and clothing.	Record and list all food you consumed yesterday. Compare it to the guidelines for a healthy diet.	Review the warm-up routine used prior to football games. Determine the impact on the body and potential impact on the game.	Review the school rules. Determine which would be best eliminated. Provide rationale.	Create a classification system to organize your comic book collection.
Procedural (Knowledge of methods and procedures)	List the steps used when making a sandwich.	Explain how to add two fractions with unlike denominators.	Solve the equation $2x = 748$.	Explain why this answer is incorrect.	Read the movie critique. Compare it to your analysis and make recommendations for change.	Using the ingredients provided to you, create a recipe. Make the food.
Metacognitive (Knowledge of one's own thinking and the thinking of others; strategic knowledge)	What is the place you find best to do homework?	Explain why the author used the setting for the story.	Determine a plan to help you study for your college entrance exam.	What was the main character thinking when he fled the country?	Read the sequence of events described in the article. Why did the author not describe events sequentially?	Design a method to help evaluate the thinking of others.

1. Identify the standards and the content to teach.

2. Determine what students need to know and do according to the standards.

3. Identify the questions to ask to ensure students gain the desired knowledge and skills.

These steps don't complete the design process but instead set the stage for the assessment-development and lesson-design stages that would follow this process. Figure 2.11 provides an example of these steps using a literature lesson. The template helps teachers create questions that evaluate the standard and ensure that students use higher-order thinking skills to demonstrate their understanding. Bloom's taxonomy can guide question development so that students can achieve the learning targets. Developing questions early in the lesson-design process ensures that they are directly related to the standards and learning targets. You can use the questions as tools for classroom discussion, group work, or individual assessments.

Standards	Identify the theme of a story, providing insights and specific examples from the text.		
Lesson Targets	• Students will know details in a story and be able to communicate how events impact the story. • Students will be able to identify the theme and support their beliefs with evidence from the story.		
Question Design	1. Who were the main characters in the story? 2. Where did the story mostly take place? 3. When did the story take place?	❑ Creating ❑ Evaluating ❑ Analyzing	❑ Applying ❑ Understanding ☑ Remembering
	4. In your own words, what are the main events of the story?	❑ Creating ❑ Evaluating ❑ Analyzing	❑ Applying ☑ Understanding ❑ Remembering
	5. What is the theme of the story?	❑ Creating ❑ Evaluating ❑ Analyzing	☑ Applying ❑ Understanding ❑ Remembering
	6. What evidence in the story supports the theme you have identified?	❑ Creating ❑ Evaluating ☑ Analyzing	❑ Applying ❑ Understanding ❑ Remembering
	7. What techniques did the author use to develop the theme throughout the story?	❑ Creating ☑ Evaluating ❑ Analyzing	❑ Applying ❑ Understanding ❑ Remembering
	8. Assign a new trait to the main character. How can the trait support or contradict the theme?	☑ Creating ❑ Evaluating ❑ Analyzing	❑ Applying ❑ Understanding ❑ Remembering

Figure 2.11: Question identification template.

Visit **go.SolutionTree.com/instruction** *for a free reproducible version of this figure.*

Although all standards may not require questions at all levels of the taxonomy in order to increase cognitive engagement, create a balance so that some questions build a foundation and others extend and apply skills and concepts.

Notice that in figure 2.11, multiple questions apply to the lowest level of Bloom's taxonomy. These questions determine whether students have read and know the basic information in the story. Students will need this foundation to adequately address the questions at higher levels of application and understanding. Each level of Bloom's taxonomy's cognitive domain is represented on the right side of the template in order to easily visualize which questions are at each of the various levels. Questions can be added to strengthen student understanding and level of performance at any or all levels of thinking. Questions, when more generic in nature like those in this example, can be used repeatedly with different pieces of literature. Students will strengthen their ability to perform the standards as a result of the multiple opportunities to demonstrate their understanding at various times throughout the school year. Questions designed with Bloom's taxonomy in mind can scaffold learning to lead students from the simple to the complex. Questions that challenge students and require them to think, process, struggle, and discover can also be used to initiate discussion. In other words, students don't need to work through all levels of questions in order to reach the top but can be challenged to reach higher levels without responding to several lower-level questions. However, if you're unsure whether students have the background necessary to respond to higher levels of questions, lower levels serve to scaffold thinking and lead students to more sophisticated thought (Walsh & Sattes, 2005).

Tools such as verb lists are extremely helpful when designing questions. They prompt thought and help us consider student-learning targets as related to reasoning. Increased depth in questioning helps not only evaluate students' ability but commit their understanding to long-term memory supporting the consistent ability to apply, analyze, evaluate, and create. Table 2.3 (page 30) provides an example of connections between Bloom's taxonomy domains and verbs.

As is evident in table 2.3, verbs may be associated with more than one domain. How we use the verbs distinguishes the level of questioning they promote. For example, if we ask students to compare the numbers 10,010 and 10,100, we are asking that they apply their knowledge of place value. However, if we ask students to compare two historical characters, we are asking them to evaluate the traits of each individual and analyze their findings.

When teachers use it in the classroom, Bloom's taxonomy promotes higher-order thinking. Question design becomes part of the lesson-planning process because the domains identify how teachers will evaluate learning. Questions tie to the standards, content, and learning targets. The cognitive domains ensure that students go beyond the lowest level of thought. Higher-level questions increase the students' depth of learning and often center on the application of knowledge in ways that will solidify understanding (Marzano, Pickering, & Pollock, 2001). Chapter 3 tells you more about using Bloom's taxonomy for assessment. Bloom's taxonomy helps you design questions at increased levels of sophistication. Webb's Depth of Knowledge is a tool for evaluating the cognitive complexity required by a standard and for evaluating existing questions to determine the rigor required to respond to them.

Table 2.3: Verbs Change Domain

Domain	Verb
Remember (Access knowledge from memory.)	define, describe, identify, label, list, match, memorize, name, remember, recall, recite, record, repeat, reproduce, select, state
Understand (Make meaning of information.)	clarify, demonstrate, describe, detail, expand, explain, express, retell, summarize
Apply (Use information in various situations.)	calculate, compare, contrast, convert, demonstrate, determine, elaborate, solve
Analyze (Relate parts to the whole; break apart information to investigate.)	analyze, categorize, classify, compare, confirm, contrast, diagram, disprove, identify, illustrate, infer, outline, prove, simplify
Evaluate (Make judgments based on evidence.)	criticize, decide, defend, discover, evaluate, explain, interpret, judge, justify, predict, prove
Create (Produce something original or recreate something known.)	construct, create, design, develop, devise, extrapolate, generate, illustrate, improve, judge, produce

Connecting Webb's Depth of Knowledge Framework to Higher-Order Thinking Skills

In the 1990s, when Norman Webb was a senior researcher at the Wisconsin Center for Education Research, he developed the Depth of Knowledge (DOK), which provides a framework for viewing standards and assessment items according to their cognitive complexity. Webb developed the DOK framework because he recognized the need for a system that looked at educational standards through the lens of complexity. DOK has gained popularity in its use for evaluating the sophistication of state test items. Visit **go.SolutionTree.com/instruction** to read an interview with Webb, who clarifies some misunderstandings around DOK.

Webb points out that complexity and difficulty are two different things: an item can be difficult without being complex. Webb cites the example of a gentleman named Marc Umile, who in March of 2006 recited pi to over 15,000 digits. Although memorizing these digits is a difficult task, it did not require advanced thought or critical thinking. Analyzing information or comparing multiple sources requires more cognitive engagement—it is complex (Webb, 1997, 1999).

Introduction and Terminology

Webb (1997, 1999) identifies four levels of complexity via state standard reviews. The DOK framework is not a consecutive set of steps; its four levels are not in order. Each level considers the knowledge one needs to complete a task while also taking into account the question's sophistication and the number of steps one must take in order to identify an outcome. Content complexity can be associated with the number of parts in a task, the amount of prior knowledge needed to understand and perform, and the processing of concepts and skills needed to attain the standard.

The levels of DOK encompass the levels of sophistication of all standards. Examples are provided later in the chapter. Table 2.4 provides further insight into the four DOK levels.

Table 2.4: Depth of Knowledge Levels and Characteristics

DOK Level	Characteristics
Level 1: Recall and Reproduction	Students recall or reproduce information or carry out a known procedure.
Level 2: Skills and Concepts	Students use information or conceptual knowledge to solve a problem. Often two or more steps are necessary to complete a task.
Level 3: Strategic Thinking	Students reason and develop a plan that will lead to a solution. Multiple steps or sources are an indication of the need for strategic thinking. There may be multiple answers to a problem.
Level 4: Extended Thinking	Students think and investigate over time. Students need to review multiple facets of a problem.

DOK Levels in Action

Because the initial purpose of DOK was to assign a level of complexity to a standard, it serves us well to look at a few examples. Webb (1997, 1999) emphasizes the concept of cognitive complexity and asks that we seek caution in looking at verbs alone to judge complexity. For example, the following two statements use the same verb but have different complexity levels: (1) create a clay duplicate of this statue and (2) create a new, effective solution to the problem faced by the main character. In example one, students are simply copying something that exists—even though the verb could promote advanced thinking. In example two, the student is required to use knowledge to design an original response. We need to look at the intended outcome of the standard in order to get a match to a DOK level.

Figure 2.12 (page 32) shares an example of common language used within many state and national standards so examples are available at each DOK level. When assigning DOK levels to standards, Webb (1997, 1999) suggests that it be a collaborative effort in a school or district. The level assigned could be different depending on group or individual interpretation of the standard.

DOK Level	Sample English Language Arts Standard	Reason
Level 1: Recall and Reproduction	**Informational Text, Key Ideas and Details, Grade 5** Quote accurately from a text when explaining what the text says explicitly and when drawing inferences from the text.	Recalling or reproducing information
Level 2: Skills and Concepts	**Informational Text, Integration of Knowledge and Ideas, Grade 2** Explain how specific images (for example, a diagram showing how a machine works) contribute to and clarify a text.	Interpreting information to determine how it contributes to a text
Level 3: Strategic Thinking	**Literature, Key Ideas and Details, Grade 5** Compare and contrast two or more characters, settings, or events in a story or drama, drawing on specific details in the text.	Using reasoning to compare multiple pieces of information
Level 4: Extended Thinking	**Literature, Craft and Structure, Grade 4** Compare and contrast the point of view from which different stories are narrated, including the difference between first- and third-person narrations.	Making comparisons across texts, requiring additional time and thought to synthesize and consolidate the information

Source for Standards: NGA & CCSSO, 2010a.

Figure 2.12: Depth of Knowledge levels assigned to standards—sample.

*Visit **go.SolutionTree.com/instruction** for a free reproducible version of this figure.*

DOK levels evaluate standards, but consider assigning them to tasks as well. If a standard is written at a Level 3, but the tasks assigned are at a Level 1, we will likely not provide students with the level of understanding necessary to completely master the standard. Figure 2.13 provides a sample task at increased levels of complexity.

DOK Level	English Language Arts Example
Level 1: Recall and Reproduction	Who is the main character in the story?
Level 2: Skills and Concepts	Identify the theme in the story. Provide evidence from the story to support the theme you have chosen.

Level 3: Strategic Thinking	Compare the Wicked Witch from *The Wonderful Wizard of Oz* to the Queen of Hearts in *Alice's Adventures in Wonderland*. How are they similar and how are they different? Provide evidence.
Level 4: Extended Thinking	Read two different stories by the same author. Describe similarities and differences in the writing style of the author.

Figure 2.13: Using DOK in an English language arts lesson.

Figure 2.14 provides a science example. When creating and evaluating tasks, keep in mind the descriptors in table 2.3.

DOK Level	Science Example
Level 1: Recall and Reproduction	Describe the process of photosynthesis.
Level 2: Skills and Concepts	You notice that a plant in your classroom is not doing well. How would you determine the cause?
Level 3: Strategic Thinking	You have little direct light in your bedroom, but would like to have a plant. What plant would you choose, and why?
Level 4: Extended Thinking	Research and plan a garden that will adequately supply vegetables for a family of four. Include a minimum of four vegetables. Include planting times, size of garden, number of plants, cost, and potential yield.

Figure 2.14: Using DOK in a science lesson.

In Summary

DOK and Bloom's taxonomy are two systems with two different uses in mind. Bloom's taxonomy provides a common language when categorizing and standardizing assessment items. DOK evaluates the complexity of standards. These systems enable us to look at standards, questions, and tasks from a different viewpoint, yet both help us consider ways in which we actively engage our students in higher-order thinking. You can use both simultaneously. You need not choose between them, as both are valuable and purposeful.

CHAPTER 3
Developing Effective Assessments

Developing questions that promote thinking is key to enhanced understanding. One of the primary ways we ask students questions is by using existing assessments or developing our own. Providing high-quality assessments using high-quality questions is an important consideration. As a result, designing and providing quality assessment is crucial to truly understanding what our students know, can do, and are able to apply. Assessments allow us to better understand students' comprehension levels. Do they have a superficial understanding, or are they able to perform at a more sophisticated level? Can students see the connection between what they are to be tested on and its relationship to the real world? Do the assessments we use or create provide experiences that promote critical thinking and application of knowledge?

This chapter serves to support the understanding and development of assessment. In addition, it provides tools for assessment design and analysis—and examples of effective assessment tasks.

Establishing Balanced Assessment Practices

A well-balanced test uses questions from multiple levels of cognition, because the results help us better evaluate the extent of the students' knowledge. Open-ended questions can support the demonstration of understanding. Awareness of verbs within the assessment can facilitate that process (Burke, 2009). You will read more about using verbs later in this chapter.

Quality questions have a clearly defined instructional purpose and relate directly to the standards and content that teachers assess. Questions should focus on content that is essential to the course of study. To best evaluate student understanding, the goal is to facilitate thinking at various levels of sophistication or cognitive rigor. Quality questions are also clear and concise so that students are more likely to respond accurately if they have the required knowledge. A situation wherein the student understands the content but is unable to respond to the question because it is confusing fails as an assessment (Walsh & Sattes, 2005). David Conley (2014), an author associated with college and career readiness, believes that deeper learning occurs when students can acquire and apply knowledge skillfully and confidently and when they can successfully solve complex problems. Assessment design requires that we provide the opportunity for complex problem solving. Assignments and assessments work well when students are required to think at sophisticated levels of cognition.

Additionally, if we encourage a *multidimensional system of assessments*, we are likely to get a clear picture of student performance. In other words, by assessing students using multiple measures with multiple formats, we are more likely to get an accurate picture of what students know and can do. This leads to a *comprehensive system of assessment*, which provides students with a variety of assessment experiences (including methods like performance, research, or minitasks) after identifying the format that makes the most sense for the content. Grant Wiggins (2014), an expert in the field of assessment, believes that determining whether students have mastered content requires *authentic tasks*, which are performance tasks that require students to put their knowledge and skills to use in a realistic setting. Assessment results should provide us with a great degree of confidence that our evaluation of what students understand is accurate. Tasks promote understanding. When students have the opportunity to apply their understanding to new or unique situations, they become fluent and even creative in their application of knowledge and skills.

Selected-response questions, including multiple choice, can also successfully evaluate student understanding. This type of question is limited in its ability to evaluate complex understanding; however, multiple-choice questions can assess comprehension, analysis, and application of knowledge (Burke, 2009). For example, the multiple-choice format is not best for evaluating the results of an experiment. Multiple-choice questions can be taken to higher levels by asking students to select the best answer, which requires them to compare and analyze. Teachers can give students text to read prior to responding to questions so they can process information and choose a response using evidence from the text (Brookhart, 2014).

All in all, we need to look at assessment as a demonstration of student understanding. Giving students varied and multiple opportunities to show what they know provides a comprehensive picture of their levels of achievement.

Designing Assessment

Designing quality assessments is the result of careful planning (Depka, 2015). Assessment design follows the same approach as the question-design process in chapter 2. In the process, the teacher identifies the standards and content to assess, determines the knowledge and skills to apply, and then develops quality questions. However, creating an effective assessment relies on further considerations.

Clear, appropriate targets for the assessment drive not only the content but the methods. The design should match its purpose (O'Connor, 2009). For example, if we want students to be able to analyze the causes of the Revolutionary War, it may require some open-ended questions.

No matter how you build the assessment, the steps in the process are the same.

1. Identify the standards and content.

2. Determine what the students need to show that they know, can do, and are able to apply.

3. Build the assessment.

4. Design and implement the instruction.

5. Have students take the assessment.

6. Collect, interpret, and respond to the data.

The goal, always, is to ensure that the assessment does what it is intended to do. In other words, if the student does well on the assessment, it should indicate that the student understands the standards and content being assessed. By way of counterexample, a few years ago I worked with a teacher who intended to assess the causes of the American Revolution. The assessment included thirty factual questions. The content included names, dates, locations, and quotes, such as, "Who was the King of England during the American Revolution?" A student performing well on this assessment clearly had the ability to recall information accurately. However, this alone was not an indication that he or she understood any of the causes of the revolution. The opposite is also true. If a student performed poorly on the assessment, it would be difficult to tell whether he or she understood the tested content. A student may not be good at memorizing information but may fully understand the reasons behind the conflict. Memorization doesn't require explanation. If I can memorize something, I can do so with limited or no understanding of the content; if I can accurately explain the content to someone else, I likely have a solid understanding.

Align the questions directly to the desired outcome. The style of question should promote the application of understanding. In the case of the American Revolution test, the teacher may have wanted to set the stage by seeing whether students knew or could access the factual information required. The next step could have been for students to use the factual information to evaluate the causes of the revolution using complex multiple-choice questions, tasks, or open-ended questions.

Mastery on any assessment can look different depending on the complexity of the questions asked and tasks assigned. For mastery to occur, the assessment does need to measure what it is intended to measure (Wiggins, 2014). Although this may seem obvious, unless we look at the assessment through the lens of the accuracy of the match, we could miss the boat.

Rick Stiggins (2007), an assessment author and consultant, supports four keys to quality assessment design.

1. The first key is a *clear purpose*. The teacher and the student are aware of the intention of the assessment.

2. The second key is a *clear achievement target* for the assessment. What do students need to accomplish in order to achieve proficiency on the desired target?

3. The third key suggests that the *assessment design* must reflect the target and satisfy the purpose of the assessment. In other words, the assessment questions and tasks are of good quality and are clearly capable of measuring student understanding of the desired targets.

4. The fourth key is that the *results are communicated* to the intended end user, meaning students receive and evaluate their results so they are capable of owning their own learning and evaluating ways they can successfully move forward.

As we consider assessment design, we need to give thought to creating questions and tasks that are both valid and reliable. *Validity* means that the questions accurately assess what we intend them to assess. Will the test questions and tasks provide results that we can trust? Will a correct response actually indicate that the student understands the learning and content they are being asked to demonstrate? *Reliability* suggests that the results are dependable and consistent over time. If the question accurately measures understanding for one group, the same experience will apply to multiple groups over extended time frames (Gareis & Grant, 2015).

Developing Assessment

Identify qualities that you want in a finished assessment. I will show you a few different approaches and examples regarding assessment design. Some considerations will help focus your efforts during the design process to produce an assessment of higher quality. Table 3.1 shares what I like to call the *definite dozen* because these considerations needed to adequately, effectively evaluate existing assessments or create quality assessments. All provide aspects to consider in assessment design. Review the twelve considerations when creating the assessment to be reminded of the components that assist in quality development.

Table 3.1: Assessment Design Considerations—The Definite Dozen

Consideration	Additional Information
1. All questions align to one or more standards.	Selecting specific standards that the assessment addresses dictates the types of questions to ask and the skills on which to focus. If content is not specific in the standards, identify the focus.
2. Assessment has a clear focus, topic, or purpose.	Identify a clear purpose. What will this assessment accomplish? What do we want to know? The identified purpose is reflective of the standards we have selected.
3. All questions and statements are clearly written and in full sentences (except completion items).	Questions should be clear and free from any confusion that could cause students to answer incorrectly.
4. Assessment contains higher-level thinking opportunities.	The purpose is to ensure that students have a true understanding of the concepts and can apply them to new or unique situations.
5. Questions match the intended targets and content.	Consider the desired outcome of the question and match it to the question design. A task, project, or open-ended question can be beneficial when asking students to analyze information.
6. Two to three questions address the same skill to ensure students can repeat the expected performance.	If students are able to apply a skill and get the correct answer once, can they repeat it? A second similar question will provide an additional opportunity, and a third can validate if the skill can be repeated at least two of three times.
7. Assessment provides opportunities for students to apply knowledge and skills to realistic situations.	When students are given the opportunity to apply what they know to real-life situations, they better understand the purpose of what they are learning.
8. Point value is clear for each question if questions have varied point levels.	When questions have different values, identifying the value helps students to know where additional time and effort may be required.
9. Success criteria are defined. (What do students need to do to earn a 1, 2, 3, or 4?)	When different values are assigned to questions, students will perform better if they understand the requirements to achieve the levels.
10. A rubric is available for essay and performance-based items.	A rubric provides descriptors of quality. The rubric clearly defines the level of achievement required to earn a top performance.
11. A system is in place to collect, record, and analyze data.	The goal of the assessment is to evaluate the strengths and challenge areas of students. Have a defined way to collect, record, and analyze the data.
12. Successful completion of the assessment will show that students know and understand the concepts being tested.	After writing the assessment, compare the finished product to the intended targets. If students do well on the assessment, will that also indicate that they have the expected knowledge and skills?

*Visit **go.SolutionTree.com/instruction** for a free reproducible version of this table.*

When reading the twelfth recommendation on the list, I can see where some might pause and ask, "Is that even possible? Could students do well answering questions and not understand the topic?" Let me provide an example. Please read the following paragraph and answer the following questions.

Noroplastons are crucial to the identification of Monders within Gohendites. Gohendites have the ability to cure Blestia, a devastating illness, only when the Monder levels are at 35 percent or higher. Without Noroplastons, the Gohendites may or may not cure Blestia because of low levels of Monders. The discovery of Noroplastons is an advance in science because it now increases the ability to build a complete cure to an illness formerly deemed incurable.

1. *What is Blestia?*

2. *Why are Noroplastons important?*

3. *What percent of Monder needs to be present in order to cure Blestia?*

4. *Is Blestia curable?*

Our ability to read and analyze text enables us to respond to questions, even if they make no sense to us. If students were to read and respond to the paragraph about Blestia, all of them have the potential of earning the highest grade, yet we have no evidence that they understand the content. Our challenge is to create the assessment in a structure where students not only demonstrate their knowledge and skills but also apply them at higher levels of thinking.

Table 3.2 provides some valuable tips for identifying components that will help structure a text to get the most benefit from it. These suggestions are not related to the content but rather are factors that have the potential of impacting the outcome. Because we want to provide students with the best chance at success, we use a structure and framework to support that goal. As you review table 3.2, identify the practices you currently use and consider implementing those not yet part of your protocol.

Table 3.2: Practices for Traditional Test Formats

Consideration	Additional Information
1. Assessment is typed.	This is most often the practice, but sometimes when pressed for time, we might decide to handwrite an assessment. This can make it more difficult for some students to read, thereby making it less possible to answer the question correctly.
2. Assessment has clearly written directions for all sections.	In order for students to be certain of expectations, directions are needed. Consider also going through the directions orally with students. If expectations are clear, students have a better chance at success.
3. Assessment contains a variety of types of questions and no more than ten of any one type.	We want students to experience success. We don't want the style of questions to confuse students. Giving multiple formats will provide students the opportunity to demonstrate their knowledge with less chance that the question type will impede their progress.

4.	Length of the test is geared to fit within a single class period and takes no more than about two to four minutes multiplied by the students' age.	The goal of the assessment is to get the best student performance possible. We don't want fatigue to play a role in results. Assessing more frequently or spacing the assessment out over a few days can also help control the fatigue factor. (Example: 8-year-olds times 2–4 minutes = 16–32 minutes)
5.	Assessment provides ample space for student responses.	When answer space is present, students can rely on the questions in front of them without being required to transfer questions or problems to a new document. They can concentrate on what is being asked without the distraction of answering elsewhere. When the test is returned to them, they will also have access to the original questions and not only their response.
6.	Questions are arranged from simple to complex.	This practice can help build confidence in students. It can also help scaffold understanding. From a data perspective, it will allow responses to be analyzed to determine whether or not students had the basics that were needed to apply to more complex questions.
7.	Questions are written at a reading level appropriate to the students.	When questions contain vocabulary or phrasing that students don't understand, it will impact their ability to respond accurately. Questions needn't be simplified, but reading level doesn't hinder performance.
8.	Assessment includes choices. (Optional)	If used, construct choices to evaluate the same knowledge and skills. The application might vary, but the result should provide evidence of the students' level of understanding on the skill or topic. For example, if the goal is to have students identify the theme of a story, the following options could apply. • Option one: Explain the theme of the story and provide evidence and justification for your opinion. • Option two: Create an illustration of the theme providing evidence and detail from the story. Explain how your drawing is representative of the theme.

Defining the Framework

A definition of purpose is a good start to the development of quality assessments. Our job as assessors is to provide a framework that will assist a student in demonstrating his or her knowledge and skills. We need to take care in order to be clear and focused—to eliminate anything that could be tricky or easily misunderstood. This does not mean decreasing the level of difficulty or sophistication. In fact, we want to make sure that our structure provides students the opportunity to apply and extend knowledge and skills.

After identifying the purpose of the assessment, we can determine the types of questions to ask that will prove whether students have the foundational knowledge and skills necessary to answer questions that promote higher-order thinking. When we are satisfied that the questions will provide the foundational evidence of knowledge and skills, questions and tasks can be generated at higher levels of Bloom's taxonomy to encourage evidence of true understanding.

Using Bloom's Taxonomy to Build Assessments

According to John V. Antonetti and James R. Garver (2015) in their book *17,000 Classroom Visits Can't Be Wrong*, most classroom questions are at the lowest levels of Bloom's taxonomy. In fact, they state that in only 4 percent of the classrooms visited did questions reach the top two levels of the taxonomy. Nine percent of questions fell into the two middle levels. A startling 87 percent of classroom questions were stuck in the lowest two levels of Bloom's taxonomy. Antonetti and Garver (2015) suggest that even if we were to concentrate on the two middle levels of applying and analyzing, we would better serve our students. They indicate that the brain likes to find ways to apply information usefully to realistic situations. Analyzing patterns can cause students to see relationships in concepts, and to understand and organize content in meaningful ways. Even if we are not always able to design assessments using all Bloom's levels, helping students apply and analyze information is more impactful than what occurs in the majority of classrooms visited in this study. Using the taxonomy for classroom questioning and assessment development will cause students to demonstrate deeper understanding.

Table 2.3 (page 30) is helpful for creating assessments because the verb list can help generate thoughts. Consider the following questions before you develop assessment questions.

- **Which standards and content will you address?** Consider the scope of the content. Narrow the focus in order to get the best performance from students. Too broad a focus might overwhelm students and not provide them the possibility of an accurate performance. Control the number of questions and consider the breadth of the content to be assessed. The assessment must appropriately challenge yet not overwhelm. Although questions should prove that students know and understand the content, make sure that you are not challenging them to the point of exhaustion. Ask what is needed to make sure students understand. Be aware of the length and time needed to complete the work.

- **What is the desired time frame for the assessment?** Time should not be a factor that negatively influences the outcome of the assessment. As a result, you may need time beyond the identified allotment to secure accurate results for all students.

- **Which formats or types of questions will you ask for the content?** Multiple choice, matching, fill-in-the-blank, short answer, or minitasks are all possible on multiquestion assessments. On longer assessments, consider limiting any one question type so that the specific type of question doesn't negatively impact the student. If question types are varied, a student who struggles with multiple choice, for example, will have the opportunity to demonstrate knowledge and skills on another question format that better suits him or her.

- **What foundational skills do students need in order to respond to the higher-order thinking questions?** Frontload the assessment with the foundational skills. If they have been assessed previously, including them may not be necessary. However, if the more sophisticated questions require certain knowledge and skills, including them on the same assessment is appropriate. The assessment results can then help us understand if a higher-order question was missed because the student didn't have the foundation required to generate an appropriate response.

- **How can you develop questions that will extend or deepen student understanding?** A Bloom's taxonomy verb list, like the one in table 2.3 (page 30), can help with this. Although it isn't necessary to have all levels of Bloom's taxonomy represented in an assessment, it is important to stretch students to the levels of application and analysis.

In figure 3.1, in order to respond to questions 1–4, students need to remember the characteristics of the shapes and how to draw the shapes prior to actually drawing the shapes. Questions 4–6 ask students to apply their knowledge by identifying and categorizing the shapes. Because some of these questions have multiple correct answers, students also need to analyze carefully and select all of the correct responses. The final question gives students the opportunity to evaluate the statement and provide their conclusion.

Standard	Recognize and draw shapes having different attributes.		
Lesson Target	Students can draw and categorize three- and four-sided figures.		
Question Design	1. Draw a square. 2. Draw a triangle. 3. Draw a rectangle that is not a square. 4. Draw any quadrilateral.	❏ Creating ❏ Evaluating ❏ Analyzing	☑ Applying ❏ Understanding ❏ Remembering
	5. Match the shapes with all names that apply. Triangle Square Pentagon Rectangle Quadrilateral	❏ Creating ❏ Evaluating ☑ Analyzing	❏ Applying ❏ Understanding ❏ Remembering
	6. Maggie said that all squares are rectangles. Are all rectangles also squares? Explain.	❏ Creating ☑ Evaluating ❏ Analyzing	❏ Applying ❏ Understanding ❏ Remembering

Source for standard: NGA & CCSSO, 2010b.

Figure 3.1: Question identification template—geometry example.

*Visit **go.SolutionTree.com/instruction** for a free reproducible version of this figure.*

Figure 3.2, a mathematics example at the kindergarten level, illustrates how question design can have students analyze and apply knowledge and skills even when working with a standard as basic as counting to twenty. Questions 1 and 2 are most likely at the lowest three levels of the taxonomy. Students need to remember and apply the number sequence to the given string of numbers. In question 3, the students analyze a sequence and then apply their knowledge of counting to write the numbers correctly.

Standard	Recognize and write numbers to 20.		
Lesson Target	Students count to 20 and write numbers to 20.		
Question Design	1. Fill in the missing numbers. 2, 3, 4, ____ 11, 12, 13, 14, ____ 1, 2, ____, 4, ____, ____, 7 3, 4, 5, ____, 7, 8, 9, ____ 14, 15, 16, ____, ____, 19, ____	☐ Creating ☐ Evaluating ☐ Analyzing	☐ Applying ☑ Understanding ☑ Remembering
	2. Write the number sequence correctly. 2, 3, 6, 6, 7 _____ 8, 9, 11, 10, 12 _____ 15, 17, 19 _____	☐ Creating ☑ Evaluating ☑ Analyzing	☐ Applying ☐ Understanding ☐ Remembering
	3. Jaime was asked to write the numbers from 12–20. This is what she wrote. 12, 14, 15, 15, 17, 18, 20 How would you write the number sequence? Write it below.	☑ Creating ☑ Evaluating ☐ Analyzing	☐ Applying ☐ Understanding ☐ Remembering

Figure 3.2: Question identification template—counting example.

Figure 3.3 provides another example of how, even with standards that appear to center on the lower levels of Bloom's taxonomy, we can design questions that help students apply their knowledge and skills at a higher level of sophistication. In order to determine whether students know some of the rules regarding punctuation, question 1 has them apply their understanding. Question 3 causes students to use commas in a different way and then analyze how and why comma placement can be important not only to understanding the sentence but in creating the meaning of the sentence as well.

Standard	Demonstrate conventions of the English language.		
Lesson Target	Students will understand and demonstrate how commas can influence the meaning of a sentence.		
Question Design	1. Place commas where they are needed in the following sentences. James wearing his new suit was ready for the graduation ceremony. Amy's baby brother liked carrots peas squash and bananas the best. The book *Tales of a Fourth Grade Nothing* was difficult to find because someone placed it on the wrong shelf. The winter months of December January and February were Jordan's favorite months because he liked to ski.	☐ Creating ☐ Evaluating ☐ Analyzing	☑ Applying ☑ Understanding ☑ Remembering
	2. Place a comma or commas in different, but acceptable, places in the following sentences. Johnny cried the wolf he's chasing me. Johnny cried the wolf he's chasing me.	☑ Creating ☐ Evaluating ☐ Analyzing	☐ Applying ☐ Understanding ☐ Remembering
	3. Describe how the placement of the comma changed meanings in the two sentences.	☐ Creating ☐ Evaluating ☑ Analyzing	☐ Applying ☐ Understanding ☐ Remembering

Figure 3.3: Question identification template—punctuation example.

As we approach question design, we can identify the skills students need to demonstrate. Then, through the use of Bloom's taxonomy, we can determine ways in which students apply their knowledge and skills. We do this so we can be assured that students actually understand. Let's take a look at one more example of an assessment created for what could seem like a straightforward topic. The example in figure 3.4 (page 46) is intended to take the students beyond simply remembering words with prefixes. It asks that they distinguish words that start with a prefix and others that happen to start with the same letters but are not a prefix. It also asks that students apply their understanding by asking them to evaluate how the prefix changes the meaning of the sentence. Teachers can expand this assessment to a variety of prefixes using the same format to measure whether students not only remember but also analyze the differences between when the letters create a prefix and when they do not.

Standard	Decode words with common prefixes.		
Lesson Targets	Students will recognize prefixes and know how they impact the meaning of a word.		
Question Design	1. Circle the words using the prefix **re-**. replay reach rest read rerun	❑ Creating ❑ Evaluating ❑ Analyzing	❑ Applying ☑ Understanding ☑ Remembering
	2. Explain how the prefix **re-** changes the meaning in the sentences below. Jimmy visited his grandmother. Jimmy revisited his grandmother.	❑ Creating ☑ Evaluating ☑ Analyzing	❑ Applying ❑ Understanding ❑ Remembering
	3. Can a word with a prefix have one syllable? Why?	❑ Creating ☑ Evaluating ☑ Analyzing	❑ Applying ❑ Understanding ❑ Remembering
	4. Choose one of the words below that has a prefix. Use it in a sentence that will show its meaning. undo unable uncover underneath	☑ Creating ☑ Evaluating ❑ Analyzing	❑ Applying ❑ Understanding ❑ Remembering

Source for standard: NGA & CCSSO, 2010a.

Figure 3.4: Question identification template—prefix example.

The template provides the reminder of the levels of Bloom's taxonomy and helps to create the awareness that, when designing quality assessments, we need to consider questions and tasks that engage students and enable them to reach a deeper level of understanding.

Consider also the total number of questions to ask, and the number at each level in the taxonomy. You want to find just the right fit. Plan for enough questions to adequately provide the evidence needed but not so many that the assessment is a daunting task. Typically, more questions are developed for the first three levels of Bloom's taxonomy. These questions serve to create a basis and provide a scaffold to higher-level questions.

Sometimes, determining exactly which level of Bloom's taxonomy a question reflects is tricky. Use your best judgment. Questions can overlap levels of the taxonomy. The goal needn't be the perfect identification of questions at each level but to provide opportunities to reach higher levels while providing the necessary scaffolding at the lower levels.

Sentence starters spur thought and can be useful in assessment design. Figure 3.5 provides question starters and sentence stems that you can use in a variety of situations to develop a well-rounded assessment. The starters are based on the categories in Bloom's taxonomy. By using the chart, you create an assessment that guarantees a well-rounded set of questions.

Question Starters and Sentence Stems

Remember (Access knowledge from memory.)	• What date _____? • In which year _____? • Name the person _____. • List the _____. • Define the following. • Label the following. • Describe the following. • Match the definition with the word it describes. • Where did the following take place? • Recite the following from memory. • List three details from the following.	**Analyze** (Relate parts to the whole; break apart information to investigate.)	• How are the following alike? • How are the following different? • Compare and contrast _____ with _____. • Place the following animals into categories. • Explain the author's purpose. • Choose the best response to the following quandary. • Which is the better way to solve the problem and why? • What answer best identifies the author's purpose? • Explain the purpose of _____.
Understand (Make meaning of information.)	• Retell the events of _____. • Explain how you arrived at your answer. • Summarize the events of the _____. • Clarify the following _____. • Answer and provide supporting details for the following _____. • In your own words . . . • Is this answer correct? • What is a _____? • What do plants need to thrive? • Rephrase the following in your own words.	**Evaluate** (Make judgments based on evidence.)	• What is the difference between the following? • What would you have done differently, and why? • Interpret the poem from the perspective of _____. • After reading the recommendation, are you convinced that _____? Why, or why not? • Explain which solution is better and why. • Predict what might happen next. • Using the provided rubric, judge the performance. • Was the main character justified in her actions?
Apply (Use information in various situations.)	• What steps do you need to use to solve _____? • Calculate the answer for the following. • Graph the following information. • Create a chart to organize the following. • What is the solution for the following problem? • Elaborate on the following. • Compare the meaning of _____ and _____. • Use color to contrast _____. • Solve the following problem.	**Create** (Produce something original or recreate something known.)	• Create an alternate ending to the story. • Devise a solution to the following problem. • Develop a plan to accomplish the following. • Create a design to illustrate the following. • Develop an illustration that best represents the theme. • Generate a plan to respond to the following. • Produce a video that accurately provides your perspective on the following issue. • Generate three different solutions to the following.

Figure 3.5: Sample question starters.

*Visit **go.SolutionTree.com/instruction** for a free reproducible version of this figure.*

After identifying the standards, consider the following preplanning questions.

- How many and what types of *remember* and *understand* questions does the assessment need to provide evidence that students have the knowledge and skills necessary to proceed to application and beyond?

- How many and what types of *application* and *analysis* questions must a teacher ask to provide confidence that students can apply and analyze their knowledge and skills?

- How do the assessed standards and topics lend themselves to having the students engage in tasks that cause them to evaluate and create?

The last question leads to considering the creation of tasks or projects for use along with an assessment or as a stand-alone form of evaluation.

Including Specific Tasks in Assessments

Teachers can structure tasks to fit within the assessment time frame available. If you want to have students briefly apply knowledge and skills, create a task they can complete within a few minutes. Figure 3.6 has sample tasks from a variety of subjects covering a range of content and standards. Some are minitasks, which require less time to complete than a more involved performance task. Because minitasks still promote the application of knowledge and skills, having a few attached to assignments and assessments can tell you a lot.

Subject	Task
Mathematics: Early Algebra	Mark, Samantha, and Jakia are packing supplies for a daycare center. They have books, toys, and games. They have a total of 30 items. More than half of the collection is books, and there is an equal number of toys as games. How many of each item could there be? Find two different solutions.
Mathematics: Fractions	Maggie lit two candles. The first candle is 6 inches long and burns ¼ inch per hour. The second candle is 8 inches long and burns ⅓ inch per hour. Both candles were lit at exactly the same time. Which one will be done burning first? Explain your answer.
Mathematics: Data Analysis	Brittany and Zach are playing with 4 dice. They roll the dice to earn points. Even numbers are worth 6 points, and odd numbers are worth 3 points. The first person who gets to 100 wins the game. How many points did each player get on his or her first roll?

Science: Solar System Mathematics: Powers of Ten	*Planetarium Magazine* has asked you to create a visual that will help readers understand the differences in distances of planets to the sun. Using the following chart, create a scale and drawing that accurately model the placement of the planets. Use the following distances.

Planet	Distance From the Sun
Earth	1.50×10^8
Jupiter	7.80×10^8
Mars	2.28×10^8
Mercury	5.8×10^7
Neptune	4.51×10^9
Saturn	1.43×10^9
Venus	1.08×10^8

Hint:

Make all exponents the same.

Order planets according to distance from the sun.

History: Inventions of the 1800s	The educational television station has decided to do a documentary on inventions of the 1800s and would like your help narrowing the selection. Choose six inventions that you feel should be represented, place them on a timeline, describe the inventions, and briefly state why you feel they should be included. The station will use your input to determine which inventions will be part of the broadcast.
English Language Arts: Writing	Your favorite author has chosen to add a new main character to his or her next book and would like your help with the development of that character. Help the author by describing the following. • The setting of the story • The traits of the main character • The looks of the main character The more detail you can include, the more helpful your descriptions will be.
English Language Arts: Language	ST Publishing needs an editor, and it has selected you! The following is an introductory paragraph to one of its new books. Please punctuate it correctly so there are no mistakes when it is published. Amanda christopherson, author of the best selling novel, When griffins fly has just completed her new and exciting novel entitled Wilderness island. The novel is set on an isolatd desserted islend with no electricity or housing. She conquors the wild and creates a home for herself. This wild wonderful amusing and exciting adventure will cause you to keep reading well into the night.
Music: Creating and Writing Music	The high school band is interested in a new short piece of music to play during a basketball game when our team scores. Using the instrument of your choice, create and write a short melody to fill a fifteen-second time frame. Think about the piece and have the music fit the purpose.
Physical Education: Basketball	Juan is interested in increasing his free-throw percentage. After watching the three video clips of his practices, evaluate his style and write recommendations for improved performance.

Figure 3.6: Task examples.

The entire assessment can consist of tasks that require more time—as long as students have (or will acquire while completing the tasks) the knowledge and skills necessary to complete them successfully. The tasks highlighted in figure 3.6 (pages 48–49) can generate thoughts and ideas. Notice the connection to a larger context in each. The scenario is set so that students are not completing the task for the teacher but for a purpose other than school to which they can relate.

Key components of each task include a direct tie to the standards, a real-world connection, and a context that includes engagement in an activity with a stated purpose beyond the classroom. The tasks often have more than one correct answer and typically have multiple ways to arrive at an answer. Many tasks align to multiple standards. Set clear expectations so that students know in advance what a quality performance looks like. A rubric is the perfect tool to provide that information.

In Summary

Although there are dozens of ways to develop assessments, using a tool like Bloom's taxonomy can provide the structure for a quality, balanced assessment. The area of concentration within this chapter was assessment design. However, to provide a comprehensive approach to assessment, the preceding steps support our ability to create quality tools, respond to student needs, and begin again with the next unit of study.

CHAPTER 4

Ensuring Student Success With Complex Questions

Students have different strengths, backgrounds, interests, and areas of expertise. Some find the challenge of complex questions exciting and engaging. Others may be hesitant or even confused. This chapter creates equity, leveling the playing field with students of different abilities and backgrounds so that all can experience success.

In his book *How We Think*, published in 1910, John Dewey discusses the importance of taking students beyond low-level questions. If students accept the initial response to questions that are thought-provoking or require analysis or evaluation, Dewey (1910) says *uncritical thinking* occurs. If the initial response is immediately accepted, there is limited reflection. He believes that reflection means that students process and hunt for additional evidence and data to support or reject a response. Through analysis, students can accept the response with evidence or find that it is clearly absurd or irrelevant. Dewey (1910) believes that inertia causes us to accept suggestions at face value instead of experiencing what he refers to as *mental unrest* or *disturbance*. Dewey (1910) is direct and bold in his beliefs and shares that if a person has no desire or ability to respond to a question with inquiry or advanced thought, or there is no problem solving associated with thought, the person is not educated. Children, he believes, have a natural intellectual curiosity and we, as educators, need to do everything possible to support and grow the desire to learn, challenge, and explore.

Although written in 1910, Dewey's words give us direction today. If we want students to think critically and respond to thought-provoking questions, just providing the opportunity may not be enough. In our classrooms, we can support those who need it. For others, we can increase the level of challenge and promote curiosity and investigation.

Addressing an Uneven Playing Field

Our goal is to educate all students, but all things are not equal. Some children live in poverty and have limited experience to draw upon because of it (DeNavas-Walt & Proctor, 2015). Some have learning disabilities, and still others simply learn at a slower pace than other students. We need to consider what we can do to level the playing field.

Our awareness of the need to build background knowledge is the first step. When developing lessons, consider the information necessary for students to truly understand and make progress toward the desired outcomes. What do students need to know that is not covered in the lesson yet will help them understand at a deeper level? Consider the use of pictures, video clips, simulations, virtual fieldtrips, manipulatives, and other resources that can provide students with experiences that will level the playing field for some, while activating prior knowledge for others.

For example, in a kindergarten classroom, Mrs. Jones might be working on counting to twenty with her students. This could be considered a rote memorization exercise. However, in order for students to understand quantity, manipulatives can help students make the connection between a number they can count and the meaning it holds.

Several years ago, I worked with a group of students who were solving a mathematics problem. They were asked to determine how many hooves, legs, and tails they'd find in a field of fifty-three cows. I was confident that the students understood and could perform the mathematics involved, but they couldn't do the problem because they lacked the background knowledge needed to be successful. Most had never actually seen a cow, and none of the students knew what a hoof was. Providing a picture of the animal and having students look up the word *hoof* to identify it on the picture gave them the information they needed to solve the problem. Building vocabulary with students will also be of great benefit in expanding their background knowledge.

Techniques that build background knowledge can vary to meet students' needs. Resources are available to assist in the design and implementation of practices to expand background knowledge. Bob Marzano and Doug Buehl are among the many authors who provide recommendations on classroom strategies. A Google search related to building background knowledge will provide hundreds of hits. Know that the need is urgent as you consider strategies to level the playing field during the lesson-design process.

Some students require extra support, and that can begin in the form of scaffolding. Teachers have other options for providing additional support as well.

Providing Supports to Reach Deeper Levels of Understanding

How do we know when students understand? At base it means they go beyond information recall. Understanding requires us to have the foundational knowledge and skills required in a subject to apply them in ways that are meaningful. Marzano (2013) asserts that teachers can ask students questions at four different levels to progressively lead to thinking at a deeper level.

1. Level 1 asks that students recall or recognize details associated with a given topic.

2. At Level 2, students consider characteristics of the topic, which tends to broaden the category of inquiry.

3. The third level asks that students elaborate on the topic being addressed, which can take students to an increased level of thinking because they need to delve deeper into the topic.

4. At Level 4, students explain and provide supporting evidence to their statements given at Level 3.

Being conscious of and having students use the four levels can lead to thinking at higher, deeper levels.

Marzano's (2013) levels can create a response pattern for students. One strategy that I suggest includes the key words *remember, expand, elaborate,* and *supply evidence.* Figure 4.1 provides a brief explanation of the response pattern. Answers do not need to look like a four-part response because the criteria lend themselves to being combined. For example, elaborating on a topic will likely cause the students to supply evidence with each statement. The goal is to make sure that students address all four key words somewhere within their responses.

Key Word	Description
Remember	Students list facts about the character, event, or situation they are discussing.
Expand	Students provide more detail about the facts stated previously.
Elaborate	Students include their own thinking about how or why the topic was influenced by the factors stated earlier.
Supply Evidence	Students provide evidence as to why their elaborations are valid.

Figure 4.1: A framework for taking student responses deeper.

*Visit **go.SolutionTree.com/instruction** for a free reproducible version of this figure.*

Figure 4.2 supplies a sample response. The *Elaborate* and *Supply Evidence* steps are combined within the student response. Prior to submitting a response, you may want students to color-code or highlight their responses according to their association with each key word. You can evaluate verbal responses by using the key words. Teachers can ask students to identify which parts of the answer were associated with each key word. The teaching and use of this pattern will result in deeper, richer initial responses. Figure 4.2 uses a highlighting method to indicate that all four parts of the framework are present.

Key Word	Description
Remember	In the story, the main character was Matta Dogwood. She was born on May 17, 2000. She has long red hair that gets tangled easily. She likes baseball and is a pitcher on her school team.
Expand Elaborate Supply Evidence	Matta has an older brother named Jordan who teases her a lot. Although he probably wouldn't tell her, he respects her athletic ability and enjoys watching her play. This is obvious because of his attendance at each of her games and the way he talks to his friend about the quality of the pitches she throws when the batter swings and misses. Matta appears to be having a tough year personally. Her best friend, Jakia, moved, and this has caused Matta to feel a little lost in her normal routines. She enjoyed going to the mall on Saturdays, but she always went with Jakia. Now she spends a lot of time sitting at home on weekends. She knows her teammates would love her to go out with them because they are always inviting her. In time she may decide to do that, but right now she seems to be mourning the loss so she stays home. She thinks about the fun she could be having with her teammates, but indicates that she just needs a little more time to get used to being without Jakia.

Figure 4.2: Sample framework for taking student responses deeper.

Students can use this pattern frequently when responding to literature, to events in social studies, to topics in science, and beyond. If students learn the pattern, the expectation of a detailed and comprehensive response becomes automatic. Students know and respond at a more sophisticated level because the expectation is clear. The template can help students remember and use the pattern until the components are internalized. The end goal, however, is to have students provide responses that include the four categories without using the template. As time goes on, the use of the format may require an occasional spot check.

Using a framework provides students with a structure that helps them clarify their thoughts. Teaching the vocabulary and components associated with the framework provides students with a foundation that promotes quality responses.

Using Questions to Differentiate Student Assignments

All students don't come to us with the same strengths or abilities, yet our standards set the same expectations for all students. If we work from the mindset that fair means doing the same thing with all students, some will not succeed, and perhaps others will not be challenged. We need to provide all students in our classrooms with opportunities to meet the standards. So how can we use the questions we ask to meet student needs yet challenge them to grow and succeed at higher levels of success?

Figure 4.3 illustrates a task that assesses the identified standard. The task situation is identical for students. The difference comes in how they accomplish the task. Basically, the difficulty of the task is different due to the shape students use. However, both tasks offer a degree of complexity. The teacher could select the task he or she feels is appropriate for the student, or may offer the student the option of either task. Additional support can also be offered in the form of procedures, graphic organizers, and rubrics. None of these supports change the standard or modify the standard's achievement level.

Standard: Apply the area and perimeter formulas in real-world and mathematical problems.

Task: Mrs. Rynders is building a new home, and the architect has designed the home to be an unusual shape. The contractor is ready to order flooring but is finding that he doesn't know how to determine how many square feet are required for the entire house. Please help out by finding the square footage of the building.

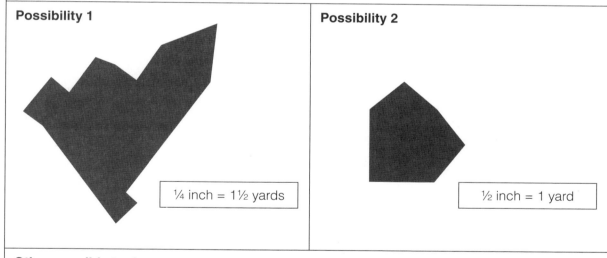

Possibility 1

¼ inch = 1½ yards

Possibility 2

½ inch = 1 yard

Other possible tools:

Provide a list of procedures to support those who might struggle.

Design a graphic organizer for students to use when documenting their work.

Provide a checklist of items that need to be included.

Provide the same rubric to students whether completing possibility 1 or 2.

Source for standard: NGA & CCSSO, 2010b.

Figure 4.3: Differentiation example 1—mathematics.

Figure 4.4 provides an example in reading using the levels of Bloom's taxonomy. The questions progressively increase in sophistication. All questions address the standard being measured. Although differentiated, completing the assignment will provide all students with the opportunity to not only meet the standard but engage in higher-order thinking.

Standard	Identify the theme of a story, providing insights and specific examples from the text.
Question Design	1. Who were the main characters in the story?
	2. Where did the story mostly take place?
	3. When did the story take place?
	4. In your own words, what are the main events of the story?
	5. What is the theme of the story?
	6. What evidence in the story supports the theme you have identified?
	7. What techniques did the author use to develop the theme throughout the story?
	8. Assign a new trait to the main character. How could the trait support or contradict the theme?
Differentiation Possibilities	**Possibility 1** For students who excel in reading: assign questions 4 to 8. For students who perform at grade level in reading: assign questions 1 to 4, 7, and 8. For students who struggle in reading: assign questions 1 to 6. **Possibility 2** For students who excel in reading: choose one question from 1 to 4 and three questions from 5 to 8. For students who perform at grade level in reading: choose two questions from 1 to 5 and two questions from 6 to 8. For students who struggle in reading: choose four questions from 1 to 5 and one question from 6 to 8.

Figure 4.4: Differentiation example 2—reading.

These two methods of differentiation can occur without lowering standards and without providing completely dissimilar assignments for students. When developing a task as in figure 4.3 (page 55), the task itself can be the same, but the structured supports can be available to help students experience success. Figure 4.4 illustrates how providing choice within structure can differentiate the assignment according to the student's typical performance level while continuing to challenge students at all levels.

When you create assignments and assessments with higher-order thinking in mind, you can easily identify differentiation possibilities. You identify which questions all students need to answer in order to demonstrate proficiency. You determine which questions will be optional, making sure to provide an appropriate challenge level for students, and you determine the support that some students might need.

Developing Essential Questions for Higher-Order Thinking

When students need support and guidance, teachers provide scaffolding until they are able to function independently and successfully. Scaffolding promotes the intellectual movement and creates the capacity to move from lower to higher levels of questioning. In short, it creates a pathway of support to guide the learner to a heightened level of success regarding higher-order thinking skills (King, Goodson, & Rohani, n.d.). An important reason to scaffold is to help students gain background knowledge, which is information necessary to begin learning about a concept. We gain background knowledge first through our ability to store and process information and then through the experiences we encounter, both in number and in frequency.

However, although questions can scaffold learning to lead students from the simple to the complex, we can initiate higher-order thinking without always starting at the simplest level. During discussion we can use questions that challenge and require students to think, process, maybe even struggle, and then discover (Walsh & Sattes, 2005).

Jay McTighe and Grant Wiggins (2013) promote the use of essential questions to offer this challenge to students. *Essential questions* are "open-ended, thought-provoking, intellectually engaging, call for higher order thinking, [are] important with ideas transferable across disciplines, support and justify, don't just answer, [and] recur over time (can be revisited)" (p. 3). Additionally, essential questions can be timeless; they are foundational to understand what is key to the content presented. The questions help students make connections to the topic or content and, as a result, students create their own personal understanding. This type of questioning opens up thinking and helps students consider possibilities that may never have occurred to them. These questions lead to more discussion, which can even turn into debate. We can teach a topic in any way we choose. The use of essential questions can assist students in making sense of the topic beyond the factual information that is presented.

Essential questions engage students' brains and lead them to consider their stance on subjects before they delve into specifics. Through discussion, we will also build background knowledge for students who may have less experience with the topic. Designing open-ended, thought-provoking questions to initiate a topic will capture interest and create a desire to discuss and know more. These questions take students to higher-order thinking immediately. They can capture the students' attention prior to having the content knowledge that they will gain throughout the unit. For example, consider the following questions. What causes conflict? In an argument, is one person always right? How does weather impact lives? Are inventors lucky or good? What makes a game fun? How do you know when someone is angry? How do you know when a teacher is fair? What causes you to want to be friends with someone? How do you recognize danger? What is the best place for a plant to live? How do you know when someone understands what you have said? What qualities make a good leader? Are all good leaders good? Are there differences between a good leader and a strong leader? How does color affect mood? Can music impact emotions? How might this topic connect to your future?

These questions provide examples that inspire deep levels of thinking and can help to initiate discussion with a variety of topics. They are written using vocabulary words that are not difficult for students to understand and require little or no background knowledge. All students could have an opinion when beginning the discussions based on questions such as these. We want to make sure that we are asking students to provide not only their thoughts but the reasoning behind those thoughts. Encouraging students to share their thoughts, expand and elaborate on what they have said, and add evidence to their comments supports a pattern that will lead to quality responses. Essential questions can help students create their own meaningful connection to a topic before a single fact about it is stated. Higher-order thinking is inspired, and all students are capable of engaging with the content.

Asking stimulating, thought-provoking questions encourages discussion and interaction among students. The question types can result in enhanced engagement and excitement about the discussion (Gregory & Kaufeldt, 2015). High levels of questioning promote deeper under-standing for both students and teachers (Walsh & Sattes, 2011). According to John Hattie (2009) in his book *Visible Learning*, higher-order questions have the potential of deeper understanding, where low-level questions support a surface level of knowledge. I believe that if we find and use opportunities to start with essential questions, we guarantee that we will get to higher levels of thought. This is not to say that the low-level basics are unimportant. After all, they can lay the groundwork for understanding standards and content while students acquire foundational knowl-edge and skills. However, beginning with high levels of cognitive engagement sets the stage for what is to come. I also suggest revisiting the same essential questions after the unit of study and tying the initial questions to the new learning that has taken place.

Using the KISS Principle

We started this chapter by identifying that there are some students who lack the background knowledge required to be successful in school unless we provide supports to create a level playing field. While I acknowledge the crucial need to increase vocabulary and build background knowl-edge, I suggest that asking for simplicity of vocabulary yet sophistication of thought can also help us establish a foundation that promotes higher-level thinking independent of the other strategies we need to employ. (This includes the use of the Bloom's taxonomy verb list shared in table 2.3, page 30.) Students need to know the meaning of the words before we use them to assess.

How do we keep it simple, silly (KISS)? The length of the questions we use and the vocabulary within them can support or negatively impact a student's ability to respond. This is not to say that we don't want to increase student vocabulary within our instruction. It also does not indicate that we want to avoid content-specific vocabulary once we are confident that students know and understand the words we are using. It does mean, however, that we want to structure questions in such a way that if students understand the content, they are able to respond to the question. To avoid confusion, we ask questions in a way that is understandable and employs vocabulary we are confident is already understood.

If we are assessing the knowledge of specific vocabulary, we need to include it. However, if we are not yet confident that students understand the words we are using, we wouldn't want to include the word in another question that requires the student to know it in order to respond. Test the vocabulary first, then assess their deeper understanding of the word as related to the content. For example, if the statements "Define photosynthesis" and "Draw a diagram illustrating the process of photosynthesis" are both within the same test, a student who can't do the first will be unable to do the second. Consider assessing in smaller chunks to help guarantee success with the content vocabulary. In this case, we would want to make sure students can define the word, and then on a follow-up test ask that they draw the diagram.

When the words that we use are not linked to the content, consider whether all the students are likely to understand the vocabulary. For example, teachers can ask students to summarize the content, or ask them to explain what they read in their own words. Both examples arrive at the same end. Consider asking students to criticize the author's conclusion or asking students to use evidence to share what was incorrect about the author's decisions.

We should also evaluate the length of our queries. For example, we could say, "Considering everything that you read in chapter 1, tell what key details are needed in order to understand the content, evaluate why these details are the most important to consider, and evaluate the best ways for you to study and remember the content." Or, we could say, "Read chapter 1 and then do the following: (1) list the key details, (2) state why these details are the most important, and (3) decide how you might best remember them." Both methods reach the same end. But breaking the questions into shorter statements helps the students know exactly what is to be accomplished without getting lost in the words.

Considering word choice and sentence length may seem like an unimportant step, but if we truly want to evaluate what a student knows and can do, we want to make the questions we ask clear and understandable. We also want to help students transition to more sophisticated vocabulary over time. Introducing new words and explaining their meaning in the context of what we want students to accomplish facilitate this transition.

Analyzing Questions for Complexity Versus Difficulty

In this chapter, I have attempted to make the case for considering students who struggle when teachers develop questions. I am not saying that students who struggle should not be challenged. On the contrary, my personal belief is that all students can learn and achieve high levels of success. The difference may be in the types of support they need and our own awareness to what we are asking and how we are asking it. Our increased consciousness will cause us to reflect on and review what can be done to support students in order to magnify their opportunity for success.

Consider the difference between complex questions and difficult questions (which is discussed in chapter 2). Think of *complex questions* as those that are more intricate, and view *difficult questions* as those that are hard to answer. For example, if we ask students to compare and contrast two books on the same topic by different authors, the task is more complicated or complex because it involves reading and analyzing pieces of information from two sources. This would correspond with a Depth of Knowledge of 3 (strategic thinking) or 4 (extended thinking), respectively. When students must answer twenty-five fill-in-the-blank questions about a piece of literature, the task is difficult because they must locate or memorize several pieces of information, but doing so does not engage the brain in the same way as the previous question.

In mathematics, we could ask students the cost of carpeting the classroom. This task is complex in that it involves understanding area, researching pricing, and calculating costs. If instead we were to ask students to find the answer to the problem $73.2 \times \$19.93$, the problem may be difficult if solved without a calculator, but it is not complex. We could say that nearly all complex problems are difficult, but difficult problems are not necessarily complex.

Why discuss this? In chapter 2, I talked about Webb's Depth of Knowledge and the role of cognitive complexity when assessing standards. This is another way to think about cognitive rigor. When we ask questions, we can make a conscious decision as to the type of questions we want to ask. We can give forethought to the rigorous nature of the task we choose to assign. If we place an emphasis on complexity, students will spend more of their time using thought processes that engage them in higher levels of cognition. Difficult problems may take the same amount of time without the deeper, richer experience. When we ask students complex questions, we get more for our efforts because we engage students in a more sophisticated manner.

When reviewing assignments and assessments, whether existing or those being newly created, identify the questions that appear to be the most difficult. Ask yourself whether it is possible to apply the same skill to a task that adds complexity to the mix. Consider the mathematics problem stated previously. When placed in the context of the area problem, $73.2 \times \$19.93$ accomplishes the same end when it comes to multiplication, but it also incorporates students' knowledge of area.

Thinking about the twenty-five-question assignment on the piece of literature, the student will likely need to research the same or more pieces of information in order to do a compare and contrast with another book. The more complex task may make the difficult assignment unnecessary.

Students may struggle if they are not accustomed to dealing with complex assignments. In order to provide support, graphic organizers can help. Graphic organizers are tools that help to differentiate for various levels of student background knowledge and past performance. Some students may also benefit from directions that include recommended steps to accomplish the task. The graphic organizer in figure 4.5 illustrates this point. Teachers can provide this tool to students who need organizational support and clear, written directions. They might also benefit from an example. Other students may want to design their own tool with which to organize the information. Providing the graphic organizer doesn't take away from the learning goals of the assignment, nor does it lessen the depth of thinking required. It is a simple way to support students who could use a bit more structure in order to experience success.

Compare and Contrast Two Books With the Same Author		
1. Determine the key points to be compared and take notes in the bottom section of the template. 2. Complete the top of the template by highlighting the similarities and differences of the key points chosen.		
Similarities	**Title and Author of Book 1**	**Differences**
	Title and Author of Book 2	

Figure 4.5: Sample graphic organizer to compare and contrast two books with the same author.

*Visit **go.SolutionTree.com/instruction** for a free reproducible version of this figure.*

Figure 4.6 (page 62) provides an example of an organizational tool that can provide additional structure and support for a mathematics task. The tool is not necessary for all students but can provide guidance to those who, with a bit of added support, are more likely to experience success. The complexity of the task has not changed. Teachers can share with students a blank template that mirrors figure 4.6 (page 62) as well. The students would need to fill in the steps they see as appropriate. They can verify steps for accuracy before beginning the work so there is a guarantee that all are on the right track. To vary the task, change the rooms they measure. Students can complete the task during the school day or as part of a home assignment where students select a room or rooms of their choice.

Mathematics Task: Determine what it would cost to carpet our classroom. Complete all of the steps. Show all of your responses and your work.	
Steps	**Your Findings**
Step 1. Find the area of the classroom.	
Step 2. Research carpet costs using the catalogs in the room. Select and record the page number, style, and cost of the carpeting.	
Step 3. Determine the total cost of the carpet. Make sure that the units of measurement you used are the same as used in the catalog. (If you measured in square yards, and the carpet is sold in square feet, change the units so they are the same.)	
Step 4. Calculate sales tax.	
Step 5. Determine final cost.	

Figure 4.6: Sample graphic organizer for a complex mathematics question.

*Visit **go.SolutionTree.com/instruction** for a free reproducible version of this figure.*

In Summary

Complex questions expand the levels of expertise and increase our students' capabilities. Simply introducing complexity will not ensure student success. We need to consider our students' background knowledge. We should think about varying levels of ability as well, not to limit the complexity of questions, but to provide the supports necessary so that all can experience success.

Essential questions provide students the opportunity to share, discuss, and debate topics that are not solely dependent on their background knowledge. These questions help students gain confidence and promote the perseverance needed to engage independently with deeper levels of content or standard-specific questions.

As we evaluate existing material and build our own assignments and assessments, questions can be viewed through the lens of complexity. We can determine if any questions are difficult, perhaps time-consuming, but don't engage the students at a deeper level. If found, retooling them to add complexity will inspire deeper levels of thought.

CHAPTER 5

Creating Standards-Based Questions and Tasks

Standards provide the basis for what we teach. Whether we use the Common Core State Standards (CCSS), modified state standards, or content group–created standards, they are the foundation of what we teach. As a result, we can rely on the wording and content of the standards to assist in designing the questions we develop. How we instruct students should be aligned to our expectations about those elements that matter the most. This includes what we want students to know, understand, and apply (Tomlinson, 2016). The standards provide clarity.

This chapter explains how to deconstruct a standard and identify its language—verbs specifically—and who receives the actions.

Deconstructing Standards With a Systematic Approach

Before you can construct questions about a standard that will help students think deeply and achieve mastery, you must take apart that standard. When working with standards, we can first consider those that will have the biggest impact on our students. Douglas Reeves (2005) promotes the use of three criteria when determining the richest standards: (1) endurance, meaning they last over time; (2) leverage, meaning they are likely to impact more than the current unit or subject; and (3) essentialness for the next level of instruction. I believe teachers can develop the same type of criteria for ensuring we concentrate on questions that matter. For example, a standard that asks that students know parts of speech and how to use them is important and needs to be taught. However, a standard that includes specific expectations regarding students' ability to write is crucial to their future. It has endurance, leverage, and is essential to all levels of instruction. After identifying the standards with the biggest impact, we can take steps to better understand the components.

In order to get a true understanding of what standards are asking, it is extremely helpful to break them down into their parts. Deconstructing standards helps us understand each of the components. The process allows us to determine a logical sequence when teaching the standard and helps ensure that we don't miss any elements, especially those that tend to be more complex or dense in design. Deconstructing also provides a format with which we can communicate the standard to our students in units that they will understand and helps us create standards-based questions. Certainly it continues to be important that we provide students with the opportunity to demonstrate their understanding of the standard as a whole. It also benefits us to measure the whole after guaranteeing that students are secure with demonstrating the parts.

Splitting the Standard

To illustrate the point, I have selected a Writing standard for grade 3 from the English language arts Common Core State Standards. The standard is as follows.

> Write informative/explanatory texts to examine a topic and convey ideas and information clearly.
>
> a. Introduce a topic and group related information together; include illustrations when useful to aiding comprehension.
>
> b. Develop the topic with facts, definitions, and details.
>
> c. Use linking words and phrases (such as also, another, and, more, but) to connect ideas within categories of information.
>
> d. Provide a concluding statement or section. (NGA & CCSSO, 2010a)

To master a standard as comprehensive as this one, students will benefit from spending time learning its parts, gaining experience and proficiency with them, and then tackling the standard as a whole.

Pinpointing Verbs

Figure 5.1 illustrates a template that breaks a standard into its parts using the Writing standard as an example. There are other ways to deconstruct a standard, but this is the one I find easiest to use to create learning outcomes, design assessments, and produce lessons. Basically, the standard is broken into parts by using its verbs to pinpoint each expectation. You will notice that each verb from the Writing standard is listed separately in the first column. The second column lists all words identified as receiving the action of the verb. The third column provides any additional information highlighted within the standard.

Standard: Write informative/explanatory texts to examine a topic and convey ideas and information clearly.

    a. Introduce a topic and group related information together; include illustrations when useful to aiding comprehension.

    b. Develop the topic with facts, definitions, and details.

    c. Use linking words and phrases (such as *also, another, and, more, but*) to connect ideas within categories of information.

    d. Provide a concluding statement or section. (NGA & CSSO, 2010a)

Identify the action verbs.	What is receiving the action?	List additional specifications.
Introduce	Topic	—
Group	Related information	—
Include	Illustrations	When useful
Develop	Topic	With facts
		With definitions
		With details
Use	Linking words	To connect ideas
	Phrases	
Provide	Conclusion	—

Figure 5.1: Deconstructing a standard on informative or explanatory texts.

*Visit **go.SolutionTree.com/instruction** for a free reproducible version of this figure.*

Using figure 5.1, we become aware that there are six things that a student must do to achieve this standard: (1) introduce a topic; (2) group information; (3) possibly include illustrations; (4) develop the topic using facts, definitions, and details; (5) use both linking words and phrases; and (6) provide a conclusion. When the standard includes the word *and,* it indicates that the students will do everything stated. For example, in part b of this standard, students need to use facts, definitions, and details, so they will be taught and given assignments to do such. If the standard includes the word *or,* there is a choice. However, students are best served with the opportunity to demonstrate both options. Ultimately, the students will put all of the pieces together in one comprehensive piece of writing.

Take a look at the verb lists in tables 5.1 and 5.2. Consider the Bloom's taxonomy verb list shared in table 2.3 (page 30). It is clear that when we use the standards as intended, the questions we create will support not only attainment of the standards, but engagement in critical thinking and application of knowledge and skills.

The standards are filled with verbs, and once again, the verbs help with question design. Tables 5.1 and 5.2 list verbs from the Mathematics and English language arts CCSS. The variety is impressive. The standards require higher-order thinking as is apparent by the variety and sophistication of verbs used. Certainly there are skills and concepts that students need to simply remember, but the standards promote the opportunity for students to go well beyond.

The completed deconstruction template has multiple uses. You can share it with students to help them better understand expectations of comprehensive standards such as this. Use the information to create learning targets so students have an understanding of the intended outcomes. Each verb supports the need for an additional learning target. For this standard, you could share the following six steps with students.

1. I will effectively introduce a topic.

2. I will group information together when related.

3. I will include illustrations with my writing when it is helpful.

4. I will use facts, definitions, and details to develop my topic.

5. I will use linking words and phrases to connect my thoughts and ideas.

6. I will provide a conclusion to wrap up my thoughts.

Table 5.1: Common Core Mathematics Verbs

apply	explain	order
classify	express	organize
compare	extend	perform
compose	find	recognize
connect	identify	relate
decompose	interpret	represent
describe	make	solve
determine	match	understand
draw	model	use
estimate	name	write

Table 5.2: Common Core English Language Arts Verbs

acquire	describe	produce
analyze	determine	publish
answer	differentiate	recall
apply	distinguish	refer
ask	draw	report
compare	explain	respond
conduct	identify	self-correct
confirm	integrate	support
contrast	interpret	tell
demonstrate	know	understand

The deconstruction can also support rubric creation. In the case of this Writing standard, you can organize the rubric in the format in figure 5.2. You can then write descriptors to identify expectations at each level of quality. Level 4 descriptor examples appear in the figure and define the highest level of quality. However, filling in other descriptors helps students visualize the steps that lead to the highest level of quality. Consider completing the figure. The criteria reflect the areas identified within figure 5.1 (page 65), the deconstruction template.

		1	2	3	4
Introduction of Topic					Introduction is clear and effective.
Grouping of Information					Information is grouped logically by topic and supporting evidence.
Illustrations					Illustrations clearly support the topic and enhance the writing.
Topic Development	Use of Facts				Facts are accurate and support the topic.
	Use of Details				Details enhance understanding of the topic.
	Use of Definitions				Definitions are effective and supply reader with important information.
Connecting Ideas	Linking Words				Linking words are well-chosen and used effectively to connect ideas.
	Phrases				Phrases are well-chosen and used effectively to connect ideas.
Conclusion					Conclusion effectively wraps up and gives closure to the writing.

Figure 5.2: Rubric design for informative or explanatory writing.

Visit **go.SolutionTree.com/instruction** *for a free reproducible version of this figure.*

Deconstruction works with any standard, at any grade level, in any content area. However, the template and process are most beneficial with complex standards. Figures 5.3 and 5.4 (pages 68–69) provide a few additional examples of deconstruction.

Standard: Compare and contrast a firsthand and secondhand account of the same event or topic; describe the differences in focus and the information provided.		
Identify the action verbs.	**What is receiving the action?**	**List additional specifications.**
Compare	A firsthand account	Same event or topic
	A secondhand account	
Contrast	A firsthand account	Same event or topic
	A secondhand account	
Describe	Differences	In focus
		In information

Source for standard: NGA & CCSSO, 2010a.

Figure 5.3: Deconstructing a standard on firsthand and secondhand accounts.

Visit **go.SolutionTree.com/instruction** *for a free reproducible version of this figure.*

Although the standard used in figure 5.4 is not necessarily sophisticated, it is packed with multiple expectations. There are nine shapes that students not only need to identify and describe but also recognize regardless of their size and orientation. In the case of this deconstruction, the template can also be used to track what has been taught and assessed. This is a kindergarten standard and will be taught over time. Figure 5.5 tweaks the deconstruction slightly so it can also be used to track when each shape was taught and assessed.

Cluster: Identify and describe shapes (squares, circles, triangles, rectangles, hexagons, cubes, cones, cylinders, and spheres).		
Standard: Correctly name shapes regardless of their orientations or overall size.		
Identify the action verbs.	**What is receiving the action?**	**List additional specifications.**
Identify	Squares	
	Circles	
	Triangles	
	Rectangles	
	Hexagons	
	Cubes	
	Cones	
	Cylinders	
	Spheres	

Describe	Same nine shapes as above	
Name	Shapes	Regardless of orientation
		Regardless of size

Source for standard: NGA & CCSSO, 2010b.

Figure 5.4: Deconstructing a standard on shapes.

Visit **go.SolutionTree.com/instruction** for a free reproducible version of this figure.

Although it might be overwhelming to create a checklist for every standard, when it includes lengthy lists of what needs to be taught, the template is useful, maybe even necessary. Figure 5.5 includes all components of the standard and allows space to track when each item is taught and assessed. This template is especially useful for standards with leverage and endurance, and those that are important over time. It can work for any standard. A similar template can track individual performance, recording grades or progress indicators instead of dates.

Expectation:		Dates Taught:	Dates Assessed:	Expectation:		Dates Taught:	Dates Assessed:
Identify Include various sizes and orientations.	Squares			**Describe** Include various sizes and orientations.	Squares		
	Circles				Circles		
	Triangles				Triangles		
	Rectangles				Rectangles		
	Hexagons				Hexagons		
	Cubes				Cubes		
	Cones				Cones		
	Cylinders				Cylinders		
	Spheres				Spheres		

Figure 5.5: Record template for standard instruction and assessment.

Visit **go.SolutionTree.com/instruction** for a free reproducible version of this figure.

Deconstruction is not only useful to simplify standards and determine how to proceed when developing assessments and assignments; the process also informs us as to the types of questions we need to ask in order to meet the standard.

Using the Remaining Language

The other language of the standards provides direction on how to design questions or tasks associated with evaluating student proficiency on the standard. In the case of the standard highlighted in figure 5.6, students need to be able to compare and contrast points of view from different stories. If we were to analyze the standard according to Webb's Depth of Knowledge, we would assign a Level 4 because of the complexity of the standard, which asks that students compare multiple pieces of literature. The verbs in the standard correspond with the Bloom's taxonomy levels of analyze and evaluate.

Standard: Compare and contrast the point of view from which different stories are narrated, including the difference between first- and third-person narrations.		
Identify the action verbs.	**What is receiving the action?**	**List additional specifications.**
Compare	Point of view	From different stories
Contrast		
Compare	Point of view	From first- and third-person narrations
Contrast		

Source for standard: NGA & CCSSO, 2010a.

Figure 5.6: Deconstructing a standard on compare and contrast.

Within figure 5.7 you will see a Mathematics standard that asks students to graph points on a coordinate plane, but more specifically, the intent of graphing is to solve real-world problems. You are now looking at the diagram from a different perspective. Look at the standard to determine the DOK level of complexity to determine the types of questions needed to assess the standard. If the standard is at a Level 3, but you are asking questions at the remember level of Bloom's taxonomy, you are not truly evaluating the standard's intent. The standard is likely at a Depth of Knowledge level of 3. When considering Bloom's taxonomy, it could fall into the categories of apply, analyze, evaluate, or create depending on the sophistication of the real-world problem.

Standard: Graph points on the coordinate plane to solve real-world mathematical problems.		
Identify the action verbs.	**What is receiving the action?**	**List additional specifications.**
Graph	Points on a coordinate plane	Solve real-world problems.
		Solve mathematical problems.

Source for standard: NGA & CCSSO, 2010b.

Figure 5.7: Deconstructing a standard on graphing.

Another Mathematics standard is highlighted in figure 5.8. This time the standard asks students to find areas of triangles, which indicates that they will apply what they know. Then students are asked to use what they know about the area of a triangle to find the areas of shapes that are more unusual. This statement would cause students to analyze the shape and then evaluate how they can divide it into triangles in order to find the area of the whole. The standard goes on to ask that students apply their knowledge to real-world problems which indicates, at a minimum, that students will be engaged with higher-order thinking at multiple levels of Bloom's taxonomy.

Standard: Solve real-world mathematical problems involving area, surface area, and volume.		
Find the area of right triangles, other triangles, special quadrilaterals, and polygons by composing into rectangles or decomposing into triangles and other shapes; apply these techniques in the context of solving real-world and mathematical problems.		
Identify the action verbs.	**What is receiving the action?**	**List additional specifications.**
Find	Area	Right triangles
		Other triangles
	Area by composing into rectangles	Special quadrilaterals
		Polygons
	Area by decomposing into triangles	Special quadrilaterals
		Polygons
Apply	Techniques	To real-world and mathematical problems

Source for standard: NGA & CCSSO, 2010b.

Figure 5.8: Deconstructing a standard on triangles.

Within the CCSS, students must frequently apply their knowledge and skills to real-world problems. This action takes students from knowing how to solve a problem to the important step of understanding how to use their knowledge and skills in a real-world situation. Figure 5.9 provides another example of taking students from knowing to doing, from working with numbers and equations to using the numbers and equations in a realistic setting with a potential purpose that extends beyond the classroom.

Standard: Solve real-world problems involving multiplication of fractions and mixed numbers.		
Identify the action verbs.	**What is receiving the action?**	**List additional specifications.**
Solve	Real-world problems	With multiplication of fractions
		With multiplication of mixed numbers

Source for standard: NGA & CCSSO, 2010b.

Figure 5.9: Deconstructing a standard on multiplying fractions and mixed numbers.

The multiple examples of deconstructed standards provide evidence that, in order to effectively design questions to meet the standard, we need to take a detailed look at what the standard requires. It is at that point where question design becomes truly linked to our learning outcomes. Our approach to question design should be directly linked to the language and intent of the standard.

Building Standards-Based Questions

When building standards-based questions, we can start with the verbs within them while simultaneously attending to the specific desired outcome. The word *solve* in figure 5.9 (page 71) doesn't help us a great deal until we see that we are solving real-world problems. However, in order to be successful at applying knowledge and skills, we will want to be confident that our students understand the process of multiplying fractions prior to taking it a step further. The assignment or assessment we build should provide us with enough information so that we can interpret results and respond to student needs.

Figure 5.10 provides an example of the types of questions we can consider for the multiplication of fractions standard. Questions 1–6 lay the groundwork to establish if students have the knowledge and foundational skills necessary to multiply fractions. Questions 7 and 8 provide real-world problems. Question 7 has students apply their understanding of the multiplication of fractions. Question 8 is more complex and asks students to employ skills previously used, including adding fractions and calculating area.

The example's suggestions provide students with the experience of going deeper than the standard by including additional expectations. The standard is addressed, yet previously learned skills are incorporated into the final question. Students may need to add or subtract fractions. They need to know how to find the area of a shape. Higher-order thinking is embedded as a result of the real-world tasks that are included in the figure.

Standard: Solve real-world problems involving multiplication of fractions and mixed numbers.

Solve the equations. Show your work.

1. $\frac{1}{3} \times \frac{1}{3} =$
2. $\frac{2}{3} \times \frac{1}{6} =$
3. $4 \times \frac{1}{3} =$
4. $6 \times \frac{1}{5} =$
5. $2\frac{1}{2} \times \frac{1}{2} =$
6. $5\frac{1}{4} \times 3\frac{1}{2} =$

---

7. Jennifer went to the store to buy some cereal that comes in $12\frac{1}{2}$ ounce boxes. Because they were on sale, she bought 6 boxes. How many total ounces did she buy?

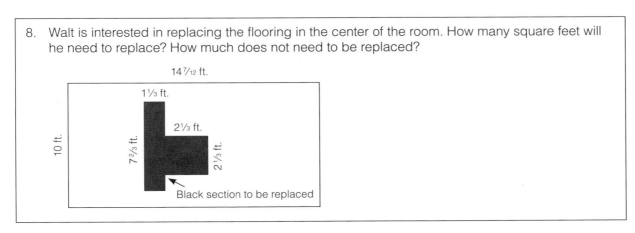

8. Walt is interested in replacing the flooring in the center of the room. How many square feet will he need to replace? How much does not need to be replaced?

Figure 5.10: Standards-based questions on multiplying fractions and mixed numbers.

The verbs within the standard give us an indication of what to ask. The rest of the standard will give us some direction as to the depth of questions required. The word *solve*, for example, is a bit nebulous even at the earliest of grade levels. A portion of a kindergarten standard asks that students solve problems in addition with a sum equal to or less than twenty. Figure 5.11 contains problems that are to be solved. There is a difference, though, in the thinking skills required to solve problems.

Standard: Solve problems in addition with a sum equal to or less than 20.	
Can you solve the equations? Use numbers, pictures, or drawings.	
1. 2 + 4 =	2. 9 + 6 =
3. 11 + ___ = 18	4. 3 + 5 + 8 =
5. Mom bought some apples and some bananas. There are 20 altogether. How many of each could she have purchased? Write an equation.	
6. Write four different equations that also have a sum of 20.	

Figure 5.11: Standards-based questions on adding within 20.

Figure 5.11 (page 73) holds questions that ask students to solve equations, just as the standard dictates. In order to ensure that students are engaged in higher-order thinking, students also are asked to create their own equations. Students are required to apply, analyze, evaluate, and create in order to complete the tasks. For some, there is not just one correct answer. This requires a higher level of thinking and causes students to apply their knowledge and skills to a new and unique situation.

In Summary

We develop questions so that students can succeed in content and process. When you develop questions at all levels of sophistication and create with the standards in mind, we increase the odds of our students experiencing current and long-term success (Cole, 1995). Focusing on the standards provides guidance for us and our students. The standards tell us what to teach, and the verbs give us a good indication of what and how to assess.

CHAPTER 6

Encouraging Traits to Attain College and Career Readiness

This chapter delves into components related to questioning that will support students' long-term success. It emphasizes college and career-readiness traits such as relating to others, communicating and listening, exercising good judgment, and leadership. When you provide students with questions that challenge them to higher levels of cognitive engagement, you set the stage for things to come. The traits that lead to student success when engaged in higher-order thinking are traits that prepare them for the future.

Investigating College and Career Readiness Traits

Relevance is important, but students need the opportunity to grow in skills and dispositions that are not content related but are crucial for success in the world outside of the classroom. Some students will attend college; others will attend trade school; still others will go directly into careers after high school. Whatever their path, schools are charged now with preparing students for college and career readiness. *Forbes* shares twenty skills that are necessary to succeed in the workplace (Smith, 2013). These skills are not necessarily about knowledge gained, but about the experiences students have prior to graduation. When you challenge students via questions, you reinforce skills that can have a long-term impact on success. You can incorporate the skills Smith shares. These skills also help increase a student's ability to answer challenging questions. I'd like to highlight a few and suggest that these skills are important much earlier and are positively tied to success in school.

- Relating to others
- Strong communication
- Active listening
- Good judgment

These skills are not on the *Forbes* list but are important to the classroom and beyond.

- Responsibility
- Initiative

The following sections focus on the *Forbes* skills highlighted.

Relating to Others

We do so much in the classroom to encourage, teach, and monitor students as they build relationships. Any successful small-group interactions rely on students' ability to relate to each other in a positive and successful manner. For some, that seems to come naturally, and for others it is a struggle. A proactive approach sets the expectation of behavior toward others in the classroom, teaching the expected behaviors and monitoring student performance in the area. Students gain experience in building relationships throughout the school day, but teachers can best instruct, support, and monitor that experience in the classroom. However, the true test comes in less-structured situations like the hallways or lunchrooms where students are expected to remember and apply the expectations. As we remind students how to act and interact successfully, we build their knowledge and skills in an area that will support a successful future.

Strong Communication and Active Listening

Most English language arts curricula include teaching and monitoring strong communication and active listening skills. Teachers explicitly instruct and monitor these skills as a matter of course. The Common Core State Standards emphasize comprehension of ideas, collaboration with diverse partners, and presentation of knowledge and ideas (NGA & CCSSO, 2010a). These standards provide us with a comprehensive approach to teaching skills that impact future success. As we know, students need to see their ability to listen and communicate not just as lessons learned in the classroom but as skills applied throughout their lives. The more successful students are with these skills in the classroom, the better the chances of enhanced classroom engagement, and the greater the possibility of the skills having a lifelong influence.

Good Judgment, Responsibility, and Initiative

Grouping these characteristics makes sense because they are interrelated. Responsibility and initiative go hand in hand. Providing support that encourages responsibility will increase student ability in the area. In order to acknowledge and support students while developing responsibility and initiative, we develop protocols for writing down assignments, creating a list of the supplies needed for class, and beyond. This information may also be posted on a webpage for students to access, which helps to grow their responsibility in accessing the information they need in order to demonstrate responsibility and preparedness for class. Certainly, we promote good judgment and responsibility in school through many different practices. We can also explicitly make the connection to students that important life skills include their behavior, attitude, responsibility, initiative, creativity, and so on.

In the book *Thinking Through Quality Questioning*, Jackie Acree Walsh and Beth Dankert Sattes (2011) comment on key cognitive strategies that are important to postsecondary opportunities. Although content knowledge is an important element associated with future success, students also need to possess strategies for responding to their personal needs. They need skills and techniques that support activities like collaboration, time management, strategic thinking, and complex reasoning. To increase their abilities to successfully perform in and out of a school setting, students require the ability to analyze, construct meaning, generate ideas, organize thoughts, and evaluate actions.

The Partnership for 21st Century Skills emphasizes that success requires students to go beyond content into applying skills and dispositions (Kay, 2010). Skills require the use of questions that promote innovation, creativity, and extended thought. Performance at sophisticated levels of understanding is necessary. Communication and collaboration skills will support success of students during school and in their lives after graduation (Kay, 2010). If all students are to succeed, collaboration and cooperation will need to be part of the learning process (Stiggins, 2005).

Our challenge as educators is to find multiple ways to design systems that will cause our students to grow their skills in the areas mentioned, going beyond the academics and into behaviors that support and extend crucial capabilities. One suggestion to accomplish this goal is the use of higher-order thinking skills and application to real-world situations.

Developing College and Career Readiness Traits in Students

Questions that promote higher-order thinking not only influence success in academics but also relate to the ability of students as they encounter and respond to all real-life situations. The ability to process information and persevere when encountering difficulties is a skill that students can learn. Recall questions cause students to memorize, yet they don't inspire thought. Students attain a new level of understanding and performance when they must evaluate, create, or engage in an activity that advances thought and deepens reasoning. Previous chapters have highlighted strategies that support higher-order thinking; now let's concentrate on growing dispositions.

How do we get students to engage in traits that promote college and career readiness? First, you need some baseline information. Ask students to provide perceptions data by completing a survey. Figure 6.1 provides an example survey—focusing on collaboration, communication, listening, judgment, leadership, perseverance, innovation and creativity, and initiative and responsibility— for periodically collecting student information. Survey data and analysis will help you measure growth of college and career readiness traits.

College and Career Readiness Traits and Dispositions Survey		SD	D	A	SA
	Please respond to each statement by marking your level of agreement. Strongly Disagree (SD), Disagree (D), Agree (A), or Strongly Agree (SA)	SD	D	A	SA
Collaboration	1. I am comfortable working with all students.				
	2. I appreciate the opportunity to work with other students.				
	3. I make quality contributions when I work in a group.				
Communication	4. It is easy for me to put my ideas into words.				
	5. When I tell others an idea I have, they understand my idea.				
	6. I am comfortable speaking in front of groups.				
Listening	7. Others tell me that I am a good listener.				
	8. When someone is finished speaking, I am aware of his or her key points.				
Judgment	9. In most situations I know what to do.				
	10. I consider several options before making a decision.				
Leadership	11. I often find myself coordinating group activities.				
	12. Others frequently ask me to lead a group or activity.				
Perseverance	13. I like tasks that challenge me.				
	14. I work to find answers even if it is not easy for me.				

Innovation and Creativity	15. I like to create things.				
	16. I often find new ways to do ordinary tasks.				
	17. I invent new games or new ways to play existing games.				
Initiative and Responsibility	18. I know what others expect of me.				
	19. Others rely on me to get the job done.				
	20. Others view me as a responsible person.				
	21. I take responsibility for my actions.				

Figure 6.1: Find students' baseline of key skills by using this assessment.

*Visit **go.SolutionTree.com/instruction** for a free reproducible version of this figure.*

Students complete the survey by selecting the answer choice that best matches their feelings and capabilities. To go even deeper, the teacher can complete a survey relying on observations of each student so that the teacher perceptions can be compared with those of the students. In cases where teachers teach multiple classes, this may not be practical; in that case, completing the survey and comparing results for select students or a specific class can help determine whether student and teacher viewpoints are similar.

In order to measure growth, you need to record and track data over multiple survey administrations—perhaps one per grading period.

Table 6.1 (page 80) illustrates a method of compiling data. The survey could also be placed in a survey tool that will compile the data for you. SurveyMonkey and Select Survey are examples that collect and chart data. Tracking data not only helps the teacher see growth in student perceptions but provides students with evidence of their progress within each trait. It identifies areas of strength and challenge so students can take action to increase comfort level and performance within the trait.

Evaluate the data in table 6.1 in two ways: (1) horizontally or (2) vertically. The recorded student numbers indicate fall, then winter performance, respectively. By looking at the results horizontally, teachers and students can review individual student progress. A vertical analysis provides information specific to how all students are doing within a given trait. For example, Randolf, the first student listed, reports that he has made growth in his ability to collaborate; he feels strong in innovation and creativity; and communication, listening, and leadership are areas of challenge.

Within all trait areas except leadership, results are mixed, with many students experiencing growth. After reviewing the results and identifying leadership as an area of self-reported

Table 6.1: College and Career Readiness Survey—Data Collection

	Collaboration			Communication			Listening		Judgment	
Question Number	1	2	3	4	5	6	7	8	9	10
Administration SD = Fall, D = Winter, A = Spring	SD, D, A	SD, D, A	SD, D, A	SD, D, A	SD, D, A	SD, D, A	SD, D, A	SD, D, A	SD, D, A	SD, D, A
Randolf	D, A	D, A	D, A	SD, SD	SD, D	SD, D	SD, SD	SD, SD	SD, D	D, D
Grayson	D, D	D, D	A, SA	A, A	A, A	A, D	D, A	D, A	D, A	SD, SD
Maria	SD, D	SD, D	A, SA	A, A	A, A	A, D	D, D	D, D	A, SA	A, A
Wendall	SD, D	SD, SD	D, A	D, A	D, A	SD, SD	SD, D	SD, D	A, SA	A, A
Emilie	A, A	SD, SD	D, D	D, D	A, SA	A, A	A, A	SD, D	D, D	SD, SD
Genessa	A, A	SD, SD	SD, D	SD, D	A, SA	A, A	A, A	D, A	SD, SD	SD, D
Gilbert	SD, SD	SD, SD	A, D	D, D	D, D	A, SA	A, A	A, SA	A, A	A, A
Monica	D, A	D, A	D, A	SD, SD	SD, D	A, SA	A, SA	A, A	A, A	A, D
Jonathan	D, D	D, D	A, SA	A, A	A, A	A, D	D, D	D, D	A, SA	A, A
Jessica	SD, D	SD, D	A, SA	A, A	A, A	A, SA	SA, SA	A, SA	A, SA	A, A

	Leadership		Perseverance		Innovation and Creativity			Initiative and Responsibility			
Question Number	11	12	13	14	15	16	17	18	19	20	21
Administration SD = Fall, D = Winter, A = Spring	SD, D, A	SD, D, A	SD, D, A	SD, D, A	SD, D, A	SD, D, A	SD, D, A	SD, D, A	SD, D, A	SD, D, A	SD, D, A
Randolf	SD, SD	SD, SD	SD, A	SD, D	A, SA	A, A	A, A	A, D	A, D	D, D	SD, D
Grayson	SD, D	SD, SD	D, A	D, A	D, A	SD, SD	SD, D	D, A	D, A	SD, SD	SD, D
Maria	A, A	SD, SD	D, D	D, D	A, SA	A, A	A, A	D, D	A, SA	A, A	A, A
Wendall	A, A	SD, SD	SD, D	SD, D	A, SA	A, A	A, A	SD, D	A, SA	A, A	A, A
Emilie	SD, SD	SD, SD	D, A	D, A	D, A	SD, SD	SD, D	D, A	D, A	SD, SD	SD, D
Genessa	SD, SD	SD, SD	D, D	D, D	A, SA	A, A	A, A	D, D	A, SA	A, A	A, A
Gilbert	SD, SD	SD, SD	SD, D	SD, D	A, SA	A, A	A, A	SD, D	A, SA	A, A	A, A
Monica	D, D	D, D	A, SA	D, A	D, A	D, A	SD, SD	SD, D	SD, D	D, D	SD, SD
Jonathan	SD, D	SD, D	A, SA	D, D	D, D	A, SA	A, A	A, A	D, A	SD, SD	SD, D
Jessica	D, D	D, D	D, D	SD, D	SD, D	A, SA	A, A	A, A	A, SA	A, A	A, A

*Visit **go.SolutionTree.com/instruction** for a free reproducible version of this table.*

low ability and low growth, we can reflect on the leadership opportunities currently available to students, provide additional opportunities, and teach students about the skills needed to exercise their leadership abilities. You want to grow students who are successful not only in the classroom, but in life. Being able to think critically and respond to questions that inspire deep understanding promotes skills beyond the academic. Students will discuss strategies, encourage and support each other, and develop intellectually rigorous cognitive habits. Effective questioning strategies not only support academic growth, but growth in the life skills that support social and workplace success.

Explicit discussions and guidance enhance growth in each of the trait areas. Consider the following steps.

Step 1: Name and explain the trait.

Step 2: Provide examples of ways to successfully perform the trait.

Step 3: Share what you expect in student performance of the trait.

Step 4: Provide the opportunity for students to use and demonstrate their ability within the trait area.

Step 5: Provide feedback.

Complete these steps within the context and content of the lesson. They will enhance and support the lesson's academic learning targets. For example, a teacher might present the following introduction of active listening to students working in groups.

Teacher: *Today we have four learning targets in this class period.*

Target 1: We will identify the themes of the stories read in our groups.

Target 2: We will locate and share evidence from the story that supports the themes we have identified.

Target 3: We will compare and contrast the theme in this story to the theme of the story you read earlier this week by the same author.

Target 4: Our fourth target concerns a college and career trait in an area that we are working to develop and increase our skills. The trait is that of active listening. When I say active listening, I mean that you are attentive to the person who is speaking. You are so actively engaged as you listen that when your classmate has finished his or her thought, you remember what he or she said, and if asked, you could paraphrase his or her thought or ideas. (step 1)

To be an active listener, I should be making eye contact with the speaker, and I should be concentrating on what he or she says and how he or she says it. If there is something key that I want to remember, I might even write it down while not losing anything else that the speaker is saying at that time. (step 2)

Today as you are working in your groups, I will be walking around the room and paying particular attention to the themes and evidence you are discussing. But I will also be paying close attention to how you are participating in active listening within your groups. (step 3)

You will have thirty-five minutes to complete your group discussion and graphic organizer. (step 4)

Lastly, for step 5, the teacher walks around the room and shares with groups examples of how they are engaging in completing the learning target. If there is room for growth, give feedback specific to the exhibited (not the expected) behaviors. At the end of the period, the teacher can also comment and provide feedback on performance relative to the whole class.

Teaching and reinforcing the traits takes little additional time yet creates an atmosphere in the classroom that is worth promoting. If students employ the traits, the discussions will be richer and group work time will be spent with increased productivity. We learn from each other. Discussions can promote student understanding and increase the ability of individuals within a group to analyze and respond to questions that originally stymied them. As the group grows stronger in its collaborative abilities, individuals can grow confidence. Providing opportunity and feedback helps the class grow in the skills at the same time that individuals are also making progress. Because students know the traits, there is no interference from guesswork. Everyone is placed on a level playing field. Students who struggle can see others modeling the trait in the classroom, demonstrating skills in the area of struggle. (See chapter 4, page 51, for ways to help struggling students.) Students can use each other as a model to guide their performance.

In Summary

Our goal is for students to be successful, not only in our classrooms but in their lives outside of school. Even at the prekindergarten level, we teach students the skills, concepts, and behaviors they need to excel beyond our scope of influence. We immerse students in all grade levels in activities that promote understanding. We provide questions and tasks that develop the in-depth understanding and sophisticated thoughts necessary for future success.

It is through the awareness and teaching of the dispositions and traits needed beyond academics that we can also influence both the academic and personal accomplishments of our students within and outside of the school walls. We don't know what their future will bring, but we can provide opportunities that set the stage for success. Dispositions influence students' performance within the classroom. As dispositions and behaviors improve, our ability to concentrate on questioning and thinking skills flourishes.

CHAPTER 7
Encouraging Student Involvement

In previous chapters, we talked about ways to incorporate higher-order thinking skills, methods to build questions, and effective assessments. We also looked at traits that influence student performance and preparedness for future endeavors. All are significant considerations as we work to expand the knowledge, skills, and dispositions of our students, as well as increase their academic understanding and college and career readiness capabilities.

This chapter works to put the responsibility into students' hands. A majority of class time is teacher led. In fact, the book *17,000 Classroom Visits Can't Be Wrong* states that students in kindergarten through twelfth grade spend 49 percent of their classroom time listening or watching. In grades 9 through 12, that time increases to 63 percent (Antonetti & Garver, 2015). This is a statistic we can work to change. Providing the opportunity for regular engagement and discussion is a start, but we need to lay a foundation that ensures our students feel supported when discussions occur.

To establish the foundations necessary for rich, active discussions to occur, let's look at ways that we can establish an atmosphere conducive to risk taking. Students will experience new challenges in their journey into questions that stretch their minds and abilities. They will want to feel sure that they can make mistakes yet experience success. Students need to believe that we have confidence in their abilities and will support them as perplexity transitions to clarity.

Building the Foundation for Successful Discussions

The classroom atmosphere that we create will support or hinder successful discussions. Classroom discussions will develop and grow students' ability to comfortably and accurately respond to higher-order thinking questions. Let's examine our beliefs about our students and their abilities prior to determining steps that lead to an atmosphere of trust and respect as we promote thinking and deepen comprehension.

Do we believe that if we promote higher-order thinking and develop questions that inspire thought and creativity, all of our students will be able to meet the challenge? Do we believe that all of our students can experience success in a classroom that promotes higher-order thinking skills? Our beliefs impact our actions. We set the stage (Brookhart, 2014). I suggest that our frame of mind needs to be absolute belief that all students are capable of engaging in questions, tasks, and activities that challenge thinking and solidify understanding. The question I suggest asking is, "What can we do to support them in their journey?" How do we scaffold their understanding and challenge thought just beyond their current comfort level so as not to overwhelm but to intrigue? The intentional use of specific strategies and expectations sets the stage.

We are in control of our beliefs about our students and our own abilities. Each year we have students who require us to use every strategy in our repertoire. We rely on our colleagues and other sources to learn more. We seek to gain from the experience of others. All of our students are capable of responding to challenging questions. For some, our support and the strategies we use make the difference between success and defeat. So how do we lay the groundwork for success?

John Dewey (1910) addresses the importance of our beliefs in students:

> Yet the teacher is not entitled to assume stupidity or even dullness merely because of irresponsiveness to school subjects or to a lesson as presented by text-book or teacher. The pupil labeled hopeless may react in quick and lively fashion when the thing-in-hand seems to him worthwhile, as some out-of-school sport or social affair. Indeed, the school subject might move him were it set in a different context and treated by a different method. A boy dull in geometry may prove quick enough when he takes up the subject in connection with manual training; the girl who seems inaccessible to historical facts may respond promptly when it is a question of judging the character and deeds of people of her acquaintance or of fiction. (p. 35)

In short, Dewey had the right idea. Our beliefs and approach make a difference in how we view students and how they respond to us. Positive interactions will lead to connections, the making of which is crucial to providing students a solid foundation. Those connections lead to student confidence, which can increase perseverance. These connections and confidence aren't possible without respect. Teachers can help establish a climate of respect in their classrooms, and that in turn boosts student engagement and participation.

Making Connections

The good news is that we are likely already doing what we need to do. We want to make the connection between the content expectations and their impact on our students' ability to successfully engage with challenging questions.

Students make sense of content through their background knowledge and connections to other subjects. Students don't automatically see relationships with new content and past content. It can be a challenge for them to realize that subjects are interconnected. The graphing and data analysis we engage in during mathematics is the same process that we can use in science and social studies.

Building an "I Can Do It" Belief System

Students need to believe they are capable of answering challenging questions. Frustration can lead to perseverance or it can cause students to give up. We don't want the latter. Create a successful experience for students by posing a challenging question. A think-aloud can initiate the discussion. For example, the teacher can state, "If I were going to respond to this question, I would consider the following . . ." Next, we might turn the discussion over to the group. Gather suggestions, recommendations, and next steps that will lead to a successful solution. When foundations support them, students will be more comfortable moving forward independently. As their experience grows, their confidence will build.

Our goal is to create students who are competent. Setting up an atmosphere of competition won't get us there. Rather than situations where there are winners and losers, encourage systems of collaboration and support. The goal is to have all students be on the same team working together. Collaboration provides a better approach where together we can promote the success of all. At the same time, students need to believe that perseverance will lead them to successful outcomes—that if they keep trying, they will benefit (Stiggins, 2005). In 1840, William Edward Hickson, a British educational writer, said, "If at first you don't succeed, try, try, try again." That is a proverb we want our students to model.

Establishing a Climate of Respect

When we respond publicly to a question, there can be a bit of nervousness around the possible result. If we are unsure of our response, or if we choose to ask a question when there is something we don't understand, we take a risk in how others will view us. In order to help students feel comfortable contributing to class discussions, it is important to honor their response (McTighe & Wiggins, 2013).

Students need to feel that they are safe to respond to questions. An environment of support and respect provides an atmosphere conducive to discussions that feel safe to the student. Sometimes as teachers, we may mistakenly think a student lacks motivation, when he or she actually may be fearful or lack the background knowledge necessary to fully participate in the discussion. If we are careful to avoid judgment while promoting engagement, students are more likely to establish a level of comfort that supports involvement (Brookhart, 2010).

As we work to build a classroom atmosphere conducive to open and respectful discussions, there are skills we can teach and additional expectations we can set. Consider the following.

- Students need to learn to be open to opposing viewpoints and treat each other respectfully when there is disagreement. The result will increase the quality of classroom discussions because students will feel comfortable in their right to share their point of view.

- Effective communication and discussion require teachers to work with students in developing the skills needed to effectively state their thoughts. This may or may not be in the standards and content we are teaching, but to promote discussions that impact learning, we need to help students grow in their ability to communicate.

- Set the stage so that students take the lead during discussions. Students can take control of the conversation. The teacher acts more as a coach during the conversation to keep it focused and moving, yet enables the students to hold a rich and valuable discussion with limited teacher input (McAvoy & Hess, 2014). Give students the opportunity to take control. All students are responsible for contributing to a small-group discussion, for example, but students can take turns leading discussion in small groups. Roam the room and listen to the discussions, providing input only when necessary. Students can also take the lead in whole-class discussions. Pose a question, sit back, and let students take the lead. Provide prompts only when necessary.

Consider ways to acknowledge appropriate discussion contributions. This will increase the likelihood that students are aware of what is considered appropriate. We can work from the frame that mistakes are not only expected but a necessary factor associated with the learning process. Understanding is a pathway that is filled with trial and error. Students will grow in their base of knowledge when they accept and expect that answers they provide may not always be correct, and that is OK. It is through discussion and response that knowledge levels deepen. Acknowledge appropriate responses, but encourage further discussion by avoiding deeming them correct or incorrect. Instead, to encourage further participation, continue asking for more ideas until the group recognizes satisfactory responses. The goal is to treat all responses with respect and have students do the same.

Establishing an atmosphere of respect requires that we set and enforce expectations, and we consistently model and acknowledge expected behaviors so that in our classroom, appropriate participation is risk free. Make it clear to students that when collaborating with others, we are expected to do the following.

- Pay attention to the discussion or conversation.

- Actively listen to the responses offered.

- Contribute by providing thoughts and ideas that support, respond to, or enhance the topic.

- Treat all classmate responses respectfully, even when we think they are wrong or off target.

- Make contributions to the classroom and group discussions. Participate and encourage others to do the same.

- Monitor your participation. Be conscious of your involvement. Although we don't want anyone to monopolize the conversation, we want everyone to have the opportunity to share and make positive contributions to the group.

Ensuring Engagement and Participation

The consistent use of questions at multiple levels of sophistication will result in the student understanding that memorization is not enough. A single answer is not the only answer. Students need to believe their answers matter. They want to be engaged in the content. They are more apt to engage when they believe there is more to the questions than a single correct response. When participation is expected, and equitable participation is encouraged, students are more likely to stay engaged (Walsh & Sattes, 2005).

In order to ensure that students are provided the opportunity to answer questions in class, I recommend a simple but effective strategy. Use a clipboard, tablet, or simply a piece of paper reflecting the names of the students in the class. While they are engaged in discussion, place a tally mark next to each student's name each time he or she participates. Invite students into the conversation if they have been quiet. Balance the conversation by being aware of those who have monopolized it. Use the same clipboard tally system when you ask questions in the classroom. It creates a visual distribution of student involvement and helps to guarantee that all are involved, whether participating in small- or large-group discussion. Figure 7.1 (page 88) provides an example of a template that works well. By glancing at the tallies, I know that I need to get Natalie and Matthew involved on a more regular basis.

Template to Record Student Engagement					
Student	**Monday**	**Tuesday**	**Wednesday**	**Thursday**	**Friday**
Stephanie	II	I	III	II	I
Natalie	I				
Luke		II		II	
Brittain	I	I	II	I	
Marcy		I			I
Matthew					
Jordan	I	I			I

Figure 7.1: Template to record student engagement.

*Visit **go.SolutionTree.com/instruction** for a free reproducible version of this figure.*

Encouraging Thinking and Deepening Understanding

Dialogue in the classroom is a catalyst for promoting critical-thinking skills with students. It not only encourages thinking but also promotes understanding. According to Mike Schmoker (1996), an educational author, dialogue in the classroom is an "intellectually enlarging activity" (p. 94). And yet, he also shares that in the average school week there is little time used for discussion. Certainly then, the first thing that we want to reflect on is how we use the time in our classroom. Do we have ample time spent in focused discussion to meet the learning expectations we have for our students? If we don't, how can we adjust and incorporate more time for this type of active engagement?

Another aspect to consider is the questions that we use to motivate student thinking and appropriate response. Students are more likely to be engaged when they find what they are learning to be interesting. How do we do that? One way is to concentrate on the use of open-ended questions whenever possible. Open-ended questions help support a climate of intrigue and increase the probability of capturing student interest. Because open-ended questions don't have a single correct answer, they engage students in a conversation of possibilities connected to the content. These questions increase participation rates because answers don't reflect a one-and-done approach. Questions that generate thought and imagination—questions that don't have a single correct answer—are open ended. Consider questions like these: "If you were the main character in this novel, how would you have treated your colleagues and why?" "How is this the same as or different from the author's approach?" "In your painting, what mood would you choose, and what color scheme would you use to portray the mood?" "What is the best way to study for a test?"

A characteristic associated with open-ended questions is that they will typically require more time for students to think. Additional wait time is required prior to requesting a response so that students can process the questions and even begin to consider multiple responses (Willis, 2006). The average wait time in most U.S. classrooms is a second or less (Danielson, 2007). When students are viewed as less capable, or perhaps when they learn more slowly, they are given less wait time. Questions should lead to enhanced student learning. Students need time to formulate and produce plausible and well-considered responses. In order for this to happen, wait time is necessary (Danielson, 2007).

Even questions that require low cognition can have more positive results if students are given three seconds to process them before responding (Stahl, 1994). Increased wait time does relate to increased achievement. It increases the number of not only the responses given but also the responses given at higher levels of cognition. Other positive aspects of wait time include things like students providing longer responses and having a greater willingness to respond. There is a likelihood of better retention. There is also a greater potential that students will generate their own questions about the topic. Some more good news is that wait time ultimately will increase the teachers' belief that students are capable of thinking and responding at higher, deeper levels (Cotton, 1988).

Consider options to increase wait time and influence thoughtful responses. Students can know that they will be given a specific amount of time prior to any response. For example, "I would like you to take a full two minutes to consider your responses prior to anyone raising his or her hand. I'll let you know when it is time." Another option might be to do a quick write with students during which they write bulleted thoughts or brainstorm ideas specific to the topic prior to sharing verbally. The think-pair-share strategy is effective as well. Provide students with time first to think individually, then to share their thoughts with a partner, and then to share thoughts with the group at large.

When designing questions to encourage student thinking for the purpose of group discussion or individual assessment, consider question design. Use clear, complete sentences so that students have the best likelihood of correctly interpreting what is being asked of them. As necessary, find ways to adapt the question to meet the student's language level. Consider the student's ability level, not to lessen the potential quality of the response or difficulty of the questions but to provide the background needed to support the learner. Determine the sequence in which you will ask questions. Scaffolding questions from simple to complex can result in building student confidence in his or her ability to respond, thereby increasing the probability that he or she will experience success (Fusco, 2012).

If there are expectations for the type of response, make them clear to the students. For example, if you have the expectation that students answer questions in complete sentences, make that known and a consistent approach. It supports students in developing a comprehensive answer. It also causes them to place their answer within the context of the question, which can help them consider the validity of their response within a complete thought.

During discussions, probe student responses. Ask, and encourage students to ask, follow-up questions. Identify a bank of statements and questions that you will use for this purpose. Through modeling and encouragement, students will follow your lead. A bank of statements and questions might include the following.

- "Tell me more about that."

- "How did you come up with that idea?"

- "What evidence might support that response?"

- "What groundwork would need to be laid to implement that idea?"

- "What other information might be useful to the discussion?"

- "Can we prove or disprove that response?"

- "Which of the ideas that we talked about can we use to impact change?"

- "How can we verify that?"

- "What alternatives could I consider?"

The intent of the practices we use and the expectations that we have during student discussions is to create an atmosphere in which our carefully designed questions can catalyze thought and increase understanding. This is accomplished through the creation of quality questions, but also through our classroom discussion expectations and practices.

Reflecting on Classroom Questioning Practices

Self-reflection helps us identify where we are and where we would like to be. Posing tough questions to oneself is required to check efficacy and achieve improvement. The self-rating checklist in figure 7.2 helps with teacher self-evaluation. You can complete the checklist at the beginning, in the middle, and at the end of the year in order to monitor how well you are using the strategies provided in this book to pose questions that promote higher-order thinking skills. Each item on the self-evaluation promotes a belief, practice, or state of being that supports quality questioning and discussion experiences in the classroom.

The self-evaluation checklist provides one data source. A second source, illustrated in figure 7.3 (page 92), disseminates data sources for more accurate information. Students can help give a more thorough perspective on how successful one's questioning strategies are. Administer the survey

Read each item. Place a mark in each check box in the right column to reflect where you feel you are on the continuum from 1 (never) to 4 (always).				
I believe that all of my students are capable of answering higher-order thinking questions.	❏ 1	❏ 2	❏ 3	❏ 4
I scaffold questions to lead students from simple to complex questions.	❏ 1	❏ 2	❏ 3	❏ 4
When introducing content, I help students make connections to other content they have learned.	❏ 1	❏ 2	❏ 3	❏ 4
When introducing content, I help students make connections between what they are learning and real-world applications.	❏ 1	❏ 2	❏ 3	❏ 4
I use strategies that help students build confidence in responding to challenging questions.	❏ 1	❏ 2	❏ 3	❏ 4
I use strategies to help students grow in their ability to persevere when questions are difficult for them.	❏ 1	❏ 2	❏ 3	❏ 4
There is an atmosphere of respect in my classroom.	❏ 1	❏ 2	❏ 3	❏ 4
My students understand what it means to be active listeners.	❏ 1	❏ 2	❏ 3	❏ 4
My students regularly use active listening skills.	❏ 1	❏ 2	❏ 3	❏ 4
My students are respectful of viewpoints different from their own.	❏ 1	❏ 2	❏ 3	❏ 4
As a result of my instruction, the communication skills of my students increase.	❏ 1	❏ 2	❏ 3	❏ 4
I often have my students facilitate discussions while I support them as needed.	❏ 1	❏ 2	❏ 3	❏ 4
I provide feedback to students so that appropriate contributions to discussion are both acknowledged and encouraged.	❏ 1	❏ 2	❏ 3	❏ 4
I encourage all students to contribute to discussions.	❏ 1	❏ 2	❏ 3	❏ 4
I keep track of students who contribute so I am sure to involve all my students regularly in discussions.	❏ 1	❏ 2	❏ 3	❏ 4
I regularly differentiate assignments for my students.	❏ 1	❏ 2	❏ 3	❏ 4
When I differentiate, I ensure that all differentiated activities meet the standards.	❏ 1	❏ 2	❏ 3	❏ 4
When I differentiate, I ensure that all differentiations appropriately challenge students.	❏ 1	❏ 2	❏ 3	❏ 4

Figure 7.2: Classroom practices that support student success with higher-order thinking skills—self-evaluation.

*Visit **go.SolutionTree.com/instruction** for a free reproducible version of this figure.*

to students; you can do so three times per year. You can compare the results from the student survey to the self-evaluation. By evaluating the results from both, you can develop an action plan that continues addressing student needs and developing student ability to participate in discussion and respond to complex or difficult questions.

Read each item. Place a mark in each check box in the right column to reflect where you feel you are on the continuum from 1 (never) to 4 (always).				
My teacher believes I can answer questions that are difficult for me.	❑ 1	❑ 2	❑ 3	❑ 4
My teacher asks easier questions first, which helps build my confidence.	❑ 1	❑ 2	❑ 3	❑ 4
My teacher helps me understand how what I'm learning is related to what I have already learned.	❑ 1	❑ 2	❑ 3	❑ 4
My teacher helps me understand how what I am learning relates to the real world.	❑ 1	❑ 2	❑ 3	❑ 4
My teacher helps me increase the confidence I have in my ability to answer difficult questions.	❑ 1	❑ 2	❑ 3	❑ 4
My teacher helps me want to keep working even when things are difficult for me.	❑ 1	❑ 2	❑ 3	❑ 4
My teacher helps students understand how to show respect for each other.	❑ 1	❑ 2	❑ 3	❑ 4
My teacher helps me understand what it takes to be a good listener.	❑ 1	❑ 2	❑ 3	❑ 4
I feel that I am a good listener.	❑ 1	❑ 2	❑ 3	❑ 4
I feel I am open to hear opinions that are different than mine.	❑ 1	❑ 2	❑ 3	❑ 4
My teacher has me do activities to help improve my ability to communicate.	❑ 1	❑ 2	❑ 3	❑ 4
My teacher lets students carry on discussions while she or he listens.	❑ 1	❑ 2	❑ 3	❑ 4
My teacher lets the class know the types of things that help us have good discussions.	❑ 1	❑ 2	❑ 3	❑ 4
My teacher encourages everyone to contribute to discussions.	❑ 1	❑ 2	❑ 3	❑ 4
My teacher encourages me to contribute to discussions.	❑ 1	❑ 2	❑ 3	❑ 4
Sometimes my teacher gives us assignments that are different from each other.	❑ 1	❑ 2	❑ 3	❑ 4
My teacher makes assignments so we learn the standards.	❑ 1	❑ 2	❑ 3	❑ 4
My teacher challenges me with the questions he or she asks.	❑ 1	❑ 2	❑ 3	❑ 4

Figure 7.3: Classroom practices that support student success with higher-order thinking skills—student survey.

*Visit **go.SolutionTree.com/instruction** for a free reproducible version of this figure.*

In Summary

As we consider practices that encourage student involvement, we need to start with our own beliefs. The confidence that we have in the ability of our students to tackle complex questions makes a difference. We also need to have confidence in our own ability to provide foundations that support our students.

We design questions that promote knowledge, skills, and understanding. It is also necessary to create an atmosphere that builds confidence and requires respect within and between our students. Both question design and the skills we encourage create a classroom that is rich in thought and filled with ideas. We promote academic and future success. Through discussion and higher-order thinking, students gain the ability to think, collaborate, and persevere.

CHAPTER 8
Growing Students' Ability to Ask Questions That Matter

Teachers initiate classroom discussions and know that, in planning, discussion is important to the advancement of knowledge and skills. In order to have a discussion that flourishes, however, teachers will need to assist students in deep levels of discussion through the use of questioning techniques. After all, the ability to question is a prerequisite for the ability to think:

> The ability to think—to be a lifelong seeker and integrator of new knowledge—is based on the ability to ask and consider important questions. How else can we gain, analyze, and integrate new information unless we can ask questions that force us to do these things? (Richetti & Sheerin, 1999, p. 59)

The result will be a classroom that is distinguished and filled with deep conversation, discovery, and possibly even debate. Students learn to facilitate and contribute to successful discussions via the teacher modeling techniques and by having regular opportunities to engage in discussion. Students become increasingly proficient at generating thoughtful questions. Their engagement in discussion results in deepening of understanding and advancement of learning (Fisher & Frey, 2014).

Although the teacher modeling strategies and expectations is valuable and will increase the student's ability to ask quality questions and engage in discussion, going beyond modeling can take us further. When students are encouraged to ask questions, they play a more active role in classroom learning experiences. Asking questions generates an increased level of interest, not only from the student, but from other students in the classroom as well. Students need encouragement, support, and instruction about how to ask questions that matter—questions that are genuinely connected to furthering their understanding. When this occurs, other desirable outcomes are the result. Students increase their creativity and problem-solving skills. They are likely to gain increased motivation. Students will grow in their ability to respond to complex situations (Fusco, 2012).

Dylan Wiliam (2011) shares another reason for providing ample opportunities to ask questions. In his book *Embedded Formative Assessment*, Wiliam (2011) states:

> When students generate their own questions teachers find out what students think is important, which may or may not match with what teachers found to be the essential learning. If there is no match, the teacher needs to re-evaluate because what the students believe is important rules the day. That is what they are walking away with as essential. (p. 69)

He goes on to talk about the necessity of being on the same page in regard to the learning expectations. When teachers provide clarity about the learning that students will engage in and create an understanding of the intended outcomes, both teachers and students are more likely to be on the same page (Wiliam, 2011).

As we work to increase students' ability to ask thought-provoking questions, we need to help them understand how to raise questions at a variety of levels of sophistication. The questions we ask set the stage. When our questions provide students the opportunity to wonder, speculate, and engage, they begin to formulate questions on their own. Students begin to identify, develop, and research questions of their own, even without being asked. They learn to create and respond to questions using facts to support their stance.

Using Approaches That Teach Questioning Strategies

While we are interested in teaching students the standards and skills, we also want to teach students how to think. Metacognition is a crucial part of higher-order thinking. Two methods are discussed in this section. Socratic circles are a classic form of educating students. Leading students through Bloom's taxonomy is another approach, as is employing templates and tools.

Engaging in Socratic Circles

Throughout the previous chapters, the message has been that the questions we ask are important to learning and that the basis for rich discussion revolves around questions that we pose to our students. In order to understand the deep meaning related to what is being taught, questions are determined specifically to attain that end. We want students to engage in discussion based on questions that motivate and engage while leading to an interaction with the content. Socratic circles can provide the experiences necessary to produce students who flourish in developing and responding to questions that matter (McTighe & Wiggins, 2013). Socratic circles create a structure to support the level of engagement that increases student ability to ask and respond to critical questions. They build a cohesive feel among the students, provide experiences that support abilities in conflict resolution situations, and promote critical thinking (Cuny, 2014).

Socratic circles provide the format for a discussion that is based on a specific purpose or text. The leader in the discussion asks open-ended questions. During the discussion, students actively listen as others respond to the questions while also thinking critically about the question posed. Students actively participate in the discussion and articulate their own thoughts and their responses to the thoughts of others.

The goal of the Socratic circles structure is for students to help classmates understand the content by evaluating thoughts, ideas, and content. Students facilitate the discussions, which are based on facts supported by evidence and not driven by personal opinion and are not intended to be a debate. The focus instead is to create a common understanding of the topics discussed through sharing, listening, and processing information.

Socratic circles are created by forming an inner and outer circle of students in the classroom. Each circle has a different purpose. The inner circle is responsible for facilitating and participating in the discussion. The role of the outer circle is to actively listen to the thoughts and opinions of the inner circle, paying particular attention to key points that surface and taking notes to remember them.

An opening question is posed which has the probability of eliciting varying viewpoints. Anyone in the circle can pose the question. It should have no clear or single answer but can be supported by the information students have read to prepare for the discussion. A question should relate to the reading and could be something like the following: The short story left me with an eerie, almost scared feeling. Did others feel that way? How did the author create that feeling? Answers are given and supported by examples. Opposing views and opinions are acceptable but should be based on evidence and the meaning of the author or source of the information. The ultimate goal is to provide a framework in which students are led to a deeper level of understanding (Copeland, 2005).

Socratic circle topics are typically based on a text. After making the selection, students prepare for the experience by carefully reading the material. The discussion is free-flowing and typically done without anyone raising hands. Students typically lead the discussion, contributing information and supporting their views with evidence from the text. When time is coming to a close, there is a reflection and feedback period during which students in the outer circle share their thoughts about the content and process of the inner circle's discussion, and inner circle participants reflect on their performance and contribution during the discussion. This is an important part of the process because it allows students to better understand how the discussion is rich and informative when participants use it well.

Socratic circles grow students' ability to think, respond, question, and reflect. Critical thinking is an embedded part of the process that engages students in deep thoughts of their own while they also actively listen to others' viewpoints. Due to the rich nature of these discussions, students develop their own questioning capacity. The effort students put forth expands their competence in developing sophisticated and meaningful questions while simultaneously expanding their ability to communicate thoughts and beliefs.

Using Teaching, Templates, and Tools

Just as we are conscious of the types of questions we ask, we can help students do the same. We can share with them ideas about purpose and balance. Charlotte Danielson (2007) indicates that teachers should show students how to use questions to extend their learning. To help students understand the levels of questioning, we can start by helping students understand *why* it is important to engage with questions that require additional effort and cognitive involvement.

Table 8.1 offers questions that students can ask themselves to help them better understand how questions differ in intensity. As the level on the taxonomy gets more sophisticated, the thinking required increases. Explaining and discussing the vocabulary and examples in the chart will create an awareness about levels of questioning that students did not previously have. The Bloom's taxonomy structure supplies an organized way of considering how we think and can use what we know in various ways. It also illustrates how our brains are engaged differently depending on the question's level.

Table 8.1: Bloom's Taxonomy for Students

Bloom's Taxonomy Level	Examples
Remember—to keep in mind I remember facts.	I can remember facts, names, places, and dates. *How do you spell your last name?*
Understand—to know how to do something I understand what I read, heard, or know.	I can summarize. *In your own words, tell me the story.*
Apply—to use information correctly I can use what I know to complete tasks.	I can solve a mathematics equation and write a paragraph. *How many square feet is a garden with a length of 10 feet and a width of 7½ feet?*

Analyze—to study closely and carefully I can look at information and pull it apart to better understand it.	I can look at details to better understand the big picture. *Describe the personality of the main character, providing key examples from the text.*
Evaluate—to judge the value of something I can decide what information is good to use, how to use it, and the effect it has on the situation.	I can look at information about a topic and draw conclusions or make judgments about it. *Name three reliable sources from which to get information about the solar system.*
Create—to design or make something new I can make something new using my knowledge and skills.	I can use my knowledge, skills, and imagination to create something original. *Give the main character a new trait and describe how it will impact the story.*

*Visit **go.SolutionTree.com/instruction** for a free reproducible version of this table.*

Give students the opportunity to learn about each level of the taxonomy. Provide them with the examples in table 8.2 and add more that are appropriate to the age level of your students and the content you are teaching. Allow time for students to work together to generate their own examples. Table 8.2 provides a few examples of sentence starters to supply students with ideas in designing their own questions.

Table 8.2: Question Starters and Sentence Stems for Students

Remember **I remember facts.**	• Where did it happen? • When did it happen? • Who were the main characters? • What is the definition?	**Analyze** **I can look at information and pull it apart to better understand it.**	• How are these things the same? • How are they different? • What do the data show?
Understand **I understand what I read, heard, or know.**	• Tell the story in your own words. • What information do you need to solve the problem?	**Evaluate** **I can decide what information is good to use, how to use it, and the effect it has on the situation.**	• How will you use this information? • What is the best way to solve the problem? • What did the author mean when he or she said _____?
Apply **I can use what I know to complete tasks.**	• What could happen if _____? • Demonstrate how you would _____. • Use the directions to build _____.	**Create** **I can make something new using my knowledge and skills.**	• Draw a picture that illustrates how the main character feels. • Write an original ending. • Create an example of _____.

*Visit **go.SolutionTree.com/instruction** for a free reproducible version of this table.*

Share figure 3.5 (page 47) if you need additional examples. Place students into groups of three or four, assign each group a topic, and ask each group to create one or more questions at as many levels of Bloom's taxonomy as possible.

For example, say students have been learning about plants. The groups consider the topic and the levels of Bloom's taxonomy and generate the following statements and questions to demonstrate their understanding of the taxonomy levels.

Remember: *Name three plants that live in the desert.*

Understand: *What do plants need in order to thrive?*

Apply: *What are the benefits of having plants in our classroom?*

Analyze: *Why do some trees lose leaves in winter and some do not?*

Evaluate: *Name three plants that will grow in your backyard. When would you plant them? How much room do they need to grow? Why are these the best choices for your yard?*

Create: *Choose five plants for your garden. What do you choose and why? What do you need to care for the plants so they thrive?*

Share the outcome with the class as a whole. You might also consider choosing some of the questions generated to use during a future class discussion, assignment, or assessment.

Encouraging students to think of Bloom's taxonomy when generating questions will help students to think, remember, and apply the information acquired from learning. Posting a chart of the taxonomy in the classroom will also result in a continued state of awareness. Questions from one group can be given to another group for its responses. Generate other ideas that will provide students with the experience of developing and using questions to deepen their knowledge and understanding. For example, give groups two minutes to generate as many questions as possible on a topic they are studying. They should try to hit all taxonomy levels. Use the questions for class discussion during the unit.

In Summary

Charlotte Danielson (2007) tells us that in quality classrooms, students are not only highly engaged in discussion, but the discussion is clearly among them. The teacher acts as facilitator without taking center stage. We enable students to increase their ability to hold and maintain active discussions when we provide them with the knowledge and skills to recognize and create quality questions. We make a mistake if we assume that students can automatically ask or answer higher-level questions (Burke & Depka, 2011). Students can drive the discussion when provided practice, content knowledge, and repeated opportunities to be in control of the conversation while the teacher serves as interested onlooker (City, 2014). Students need modeling and teaching. The stage is set as we teach students about various types of questions. Students see that questions are designed for different purposes. Some are important to measure and build skills. Others take us to deep levels of understanding. It is through explicitly teaching questioning strategies and providing students the opportunity to use and expand their skills that we create a classroom rich in student-involved discussion.

EPILOGUE
Pulling It All Together

In education, there are so many practices for us to consider. I often look at strategies that are proposed, and I weigh options. What is the worst thing that will happen if I don't implement these strategies? I follow that by wondering what is the best thing that will happen if I take the time to become familiar with and implement the idea or change. Several ideas and examples were presented in the previous chapters. I would like to suggest that implementation of anything that I have proposed is not difficult or time-consuming, yet will have a long-term impact on the lives of your students.

It will be worth the effort.

We talked about believing that our students are capable of success and can engage in higher-order thinking. They can take on challenging activities and experience success. Our belief allows us to take the next steps to challenge and inspire thought through our questioning and assessment practices.

Building background knowledge works to level the playing field for our students. We also encourage, model for, and support our students and build in them new levels of curiosity and engagement. We teach expectations associated with life skills which, in turn, benefit our classroom and our students. Our classrooms grow to even higher levels of student involvement and excitement, and our students cultivate skills in relationship building, communication, listening, and perseverance. The questions that we pose have a direct impact on the continued success of our students. Questions form a reciprocal relationship. When you pose a question, answers are not only expected, but demanded. The question-and-answer process in and of itself helps build relationships within the classroom (Peery, Patrick, & Moore, 2013).

The questions we ask cause our students to become increasingly innovative, curious, and creative. Using Bloom's taxonomy as a framework provides us with a tool to analyze assessments and create an instructional design which allows the deep levels of learning needed for students to find success. When we concentrate on question design, the intended learning is the focus. Building questions based on the levels of Bloom's taxonomy takes students beneath surface levels of learning into application, understanding, and engagement. The taxonomy conveniently provides a continuum of learning (Anderson & Krathwohl, 2001). When we combine the use of the standards with the use of the taxonomy, we find that the verbs indicate the cognitive level expected of students, and the nouns help us determine the content with which we assess. The taxonomy is easy to use and effective for developing assignments and assessments.

As we continue to embed higher-order thinking into our daily classroom discussions and activities, we change the way students think not only about questions but about our expectations. Students' view of the teacher changes from someone who wants a correct answer to someone who requires a thoughtful answer. Wait time is essential. When you effectively use wait time, you send the message to students that you are serious about having everyone think of answers. Regardless of the question level, whether it is recall or evaluation, for example, if students are not given the time they need to process, formulate an answer, and respond, the question itself matters little (Walsh & Sattes, 2011).

Standards provide us with clarity of purpose. The levels within Webb's Depth of Knowledge assist in determining the level of complexity required by the standard. You can use that information to develop questions appropriate to the learning targets. The language of the standard provides vocabulary to consider and use in question development. Quality questions result in increased understanding.

The ultimate goal is not only to write and share exceptional questions but to have students do the same. As we increase our awareness of the questions we ask and work to develop questions at all levels of sophistication, we can teach students to do the same. We are charged with teaching students knowledge, skills, and content. Think of the impact if we also teach them the processes we use to generate questions. Students can facilitate discussion. They can ask and respond to thought-provoking questions. They not only can become experts in what they need to learn but can play an essential role in the learning process itself. With students engaged in the learning process, they can better understand how to learn and what learning and demonstrating skills at a high level entails. They can better understand that they are not learning for the teacher, or for the moment, but for themselves and for their future.

To implement questioning strategies that make a difference in student achievement, I'd like to summarize by suggesting the following.

- Believe that your students can learn.

- Use Bloom's taxonomy to assist in question design.

- Rely on Webb's Depth of Knowledge to decipher the levels of complexity associated with standards.

- Design assignments and assessments that tie directly to the standards and evaluate student knowledge, skills, and understanding.

- Empower students to play an active role in their learning.

- Support students by building background knowledge through the use of graphic organizers, questions that scaffold learning, group interactions, and other methods that increase their level of success.

Just as we believe in our students, we need to believe in ourselves. We have the privilege and obligation to use our talents for the betterment of our students. We can make a difference not only in their school year but in their lives. Dylan Wiliam explains it this way:

> There is one further benefit of focusing on high-quality questions, and that is their portability. Most teachers find worksheets or lesson plans developed by other teachers to be of limited usefulness. However, high-quality questions seem to work across different schools, districts, states, cultures, and even languages. Indeed, sharing high-quality questions may be the most significant thing we can do to improve the quality of student learning. (2011, p. 105)

We have the knowledge and ability to make a difference in our students' lives. The task is not difficult. It isn't even time consuming. If we consciously consider the questions we ask in our classrooms and work to ensure quality, we will improve the quality of what and how our students learn.

REFERENCES AND RESOURCES

Anderson, L., & Krathwohl, D. (Eds.). (2001). *A taxonomy for learning, teaching, and assessing: A revision of Bloom's taxonomy of educational objectives.* New York: Longman.

Antonetti, J., & Garver, J. (2015). *17,000 classroom visits can't be wrong: Strategies that engage students, promote active learning, and boost achievement.* Alexandria, VA: Association for Supervision and Curriculum Development.

Bloom, B. S. (Ed.). (1956). *Taxonomy of educational objectives: Handbook 1—The cognitive domain.* New York: Longman.

Brookhart, S. (2010). *How to assess higher-order thinking skills in your classroom.* Alexandria, VA: Association for Supervision and Curriculum Development.

Brookhart, S. (2014). *How to design questions and tasks to assess student thinking.* Alexandria, VA: Association for Supervision and Curriculum Development.

Brookhart, S., & Moss, C. (2014). Learning targets on parade. *Educational Leadership, 72*(2), 28–33.

Burke, K. (2009). *How to assess authentic learning* (5th ed.). Thousand Oaks, CA: Corwin Press.

Burke, K. (2010). *Balanced assessment: From formative to summative.* Bloomington, IN: Solution Tree Press.

Burke, K., & Depka, E. (2011). *Using formative assessment in the RTI framework.* Bloomington, IN: Solution Tree Press.

City, E. (2014). Talking to learn. *Educational Leadership, 72*(3), 10–16.

Clough, M. (2007). What is so important about asking questions? *Iowa Science Teachers Journal, 34*(1), 2–4.

Cole, R. (Ed.). (1995). *Educating everybody's children: Diverse teaching strategies for diverse learners—What research and practice say about improving achievement.* Alexandria, VA: Association for Supervision and Curriculum Development.

Conley, D. (2014). *Getting ready for college, careers, and the Common Core: What every educator needs to know.* San Francisco: Jossey-Bass.

Copeland, M. (2005). *Socratic circles: Fostering critical and creative thinking in middle and high school.* Portland, ME: Stenhouse.

Cotton, K. (1988). Close-up #5: Classroom questioning. *School Improvement Research Series.* Portland, OR: Northwest Educational Research Laboratory. Accessed at http:// educationnorthwest.org/sites/default/files/ClassroomQuestioning.pdf on July 14, 2016.

Cuny, C. (2014). What is the value of life? . . . and other Socratic questions. *Educational Leadership, 72*(3), 54–58.

Cushman, K. (2014). Conditions for motivated learning. *Phi Delta Kappan, 95*(8), 18–22.

Danielson, C. (2007). *Enhancing professional practice: A framework for teaching* (2nd ed.). Alexandria, VA: Association for Supervision and Curriculum Development.

DeNavas-Walt, C., & Proctor, B. D. (2015). *Income and poverty in the United States: 2014— Current population reports.* Accessed at www.census.gov/content/dam/Census/library /publications/2015/demo/p60–252.pdf on July 14, 2016.

Depka, E. (2015). *Bringing homework into focus: Tools and tips to enhance practices, design, and feedback.* Bloomington, IN: Solution Tree Press.

Dewey, J. (1910). *How we think.* Boston: Heath.

DuFour, R. (2015). *In praise of American educators: And how they can become even better.* Bloomington, IN: Solution Tree Press.

Dweck, C. (2006). *Mindset: The new psychology of success.* New York: Random House.

Fisher, D., & Frey, N. (2007). *Checking for understanding: Formative assessment techniques for your classroom.* Alexandria, VA: Association for Supervision and Curriculum Development.

Fisher, D., & Frey, N. (2014). Speaking volumes. *Educational Leadership, 72*(3), 18–23.

Furr, N. (2011, June 9). How failure taught Edison to repeatedly innovate. *Forbes.* Accessed at www.forbes.com/sites/nathanfurr/2011/06/09/how-failure-taught-edison-to-repeatedly -innovate/#48e1a3fc38f5 on December 2, 2016.

Fusco, E. (2012). *Effective questioning strategies in the classroom: A step-by-step approach to engaged thinking and learning, K–8.* New York: Teachers College Press.

Gareis, C., & Grant, L. (2015). *Teacher-made assessments: How to connect curriculum, instruction, and student learning.* New York: Routledge.

Gregory, G., & Kaufeldt, M. (2015). *The motivated brain: Improving student attention, engagement, and perseverance.* Alexandria, VA: Association for Supervision and Curriculum Development.

Guskey, T., & Anderman, E. (2014). In search of a useful definition of mastery. *Educational Leadership, 71*(4), 18–23.

Hattie, J. (2009). *Visible learning: A synthesis of over 800 meta-analyses relating to achievement.* London: Routledge.

Jackson, R., & Zmuda, A. (2014). Four (secret) keys to student engagement. *Educational Leadership, 72*(1), 18–24.

Kay, K. (2010). 21st century skills: Why they matter, what they are, and how we get there. In J. Bellanca & R. Brandt (Eds.), *21st century skills: Rethinking how students learn* (pp. xiii–xxxi). Bloomington, IN: Solution Tree Press.

King, F. J., Goodson, L., & Rohani, F. (n.d.). *Higher order thinking skills.* Accessed at www.cala.fsu.edu/files/higher_order_thinking_skills.pdf on July 14, 2016.

Krathwohl, D. (2002). A revision of Bloom's taxonomy: An overview. *Theory Into Practice, 41*(4), 212–218.

Marzano, R. (2004). *Building background knowledge for academic achievement: Research on what works in schools.* Alexandria, VA: Association for Supervision and Curriculum Development.

Marzano, R. (2013). Asking questions—at four different levels. *Educational Leadership, 70*(5), 76–77.

Marzano, R., Pickering, D., & Pollock, J. (2001). *Classroom instruction that works: Research-based strategies for increasing student achievement.* Alexandria, VA: Association for Supervision and Curriculum Development.

McAvoy, P., & Hess, D. (2014). Debates and conversations: From the ground up. *Educational Leadership, 72*(3), 48–53.

McComas, W., & Abraham, L. (n.d.). *Asking more effective questions.* Accessed at http://cet.usc.edu/resources/teaching_learning/docs/Asking_Better_Questions.pdf on July 14, 2016.

McTighe, J., & Wiggins, G. (2013). *Essential questions: Opening doors to student understanding.* Alexandria, VA: Association for Supervision and Curriculum Development.

National Assessment of Educational Progress. (n.d.). *The Nation's Report Card.* Accessed at www.nationsreportcard.gov on October 21, 2016.

National Governors Association Center for Best Practices & Council of Chief State School Officers. (2010a). *Common Core State Standards for English language arts and literacy in history/social studies, science, and technical subjects.* Washington, DC: Authors. Accessed at www.corestandards.org/assets/CCSSI_ELA%20Standards.pdf on October 21, 2016.

National Governors Association Center for Best Practices & Council of Chief State School Officers. (2010b). *Common Core State Standards for mathematics.* Washington, DC: Authors. Accessed at www.corestandards.org/assets/CCSSI_Math%20Standards.pdf on date.

O'Connor, K. (2009). *How to grade for learning, K–12* (3rd ed.). Thousand Oaks, CA: Corwin Press.

Organisation for Economic Co-operation and Development. (n.d.). *PISA 2012 results.* Accessed at www.oecd.org/pisa/keyfindings/pisa-2012-results.htm on October 24, 2016.

Paul, R. (1990). *Critical thinking: What every person needs to survive in a rapidly changing world.* Rohnert Park, CA: Center for Critical Thinking and Moral Critique.

Peery, A., Patrick, P., & Moore, D. (2013). *Ask, don't tell: Powerful questioning in the classroom.* Englewood, CO: Lead and Learn Press.

Popham, W. J. (2008). *Classroom assessment: What teachers need to know.* Boston: Pearson.

Quate, S., & McDermott, J. (2014). The just-right challenge. *Educational Leadership, 72*(1), 61–65.

Reeves, D. (2005). Putting it all together: Standards, assessment, and accountability in successful professional learning communities. In R. DuFour, R. Eaker, & R. DuFour (Eds.), *On common ground: The power of professional learning communities* (pp. 44–63). Bloomington, IN: Solution Tree Press.

Reeves, D. (2010). A framework for assessing 21st century skills. In J. Bellanca & R. Brandt (Eds.), *21st century skills: Rethinking how students learn* (pp. 305–325). Bloomington, IN: Solution Tree Press.

Richetti, C., & Sheerin, J. (1999). Helping students ask the right questions. *Educational Leadership, 57*(3), 58–62.

Schmoker, M. (1996). *Results: The key to continuous school improvement.* Alexandria, VA: Association for Supervision and Curriculum Development.

Smith, J. (2013, November 15). The 20 people skills you need to succeed at work. *Forbes.* Accessed at www.forbes.com/sites/jacquelynsmith/2013/11/15/the-20-people-skills-you -need-to-succeed-at-work/#9fc460f64b51 on July 14, 2016.

Stahl, R. (1994). *Using "think-time" and "wait-time" skillfully in the classroom.* Accessed at www .ericdigests.org/1995-1/think.htm on October 24, 2016.

Stiggins, R. (2005). Assessment FOR learning: Building a culture of confident learners. In R. DuFour, R. Eaker, & R. DuFour (Eds.), *On common ground: The power of professional learning communities* (pp. 65–83). Bloomington, IN: Solution Tree Press.

Stiggins, R. (2007). Assessment *for* learning: An essential foundation of productive instruction. In D. Reeves (Ed.), *Ahead of the curve: The power of assessment to transform teaching and learning* (pp. 59–76). Bloomington, IN: Solution Tree Press.

Tankersley, K. (2007). *Tests that teach: Using standardized tests to improve instruction.* Alexandria, VA: Association for Supervision and Curriculum Development.

Tomlinson, C. A. (2016). Beyond grades and "gotchas". *Educational Leadership, 73*(7), 89–90.

Walsh, J., & Sattes, B. (2005). *Quality questioning: Research-based practice to engage every learner.* Thousand Oaks, CA: Corwin Press.

Walsh, J., & Sattes, B. (2011). *Thinking through quality questioning: Deepening student engagement.* Thousand Oaks, CA: Corwin Press.

Walsh, J., & Sattes, B. (2015). *Questioning for classroom discussion: Purposeful speaking, engaged listening, deep thinking.* Alexandria, VA: Association for Supervision and Curriculum Development.

Webb, N. (1997). *Criteria for alignment of expectations and assessments in mathematics and science education* (Research Monograph No. 6). Madison: University of Wisconsin-Madison, National Institute for Science Education.

Webb, N. (1999). *Alignment of science and mathematics standards and assessments in four states* (Research Monograph No. 18). Madison: University of Wisconsin-Madison, National Institute for Science Education.

Webb, N., & Christopherson, S. (2015). *Content complexity.* Workshop presented at the Wisconsin Association for Supervision and Curriculum Development conference, Madison.

Wiggins, G. (2014). How good is good enough? *Educational Leadership, 71*(4), 10–16.

Willis, J. (2006). *Research-based strategies to ignite student learning: Insights from a neurologist and classroom teacher*. Alexandria, VA: Association for Supervision and Curriculum Development.

Willis, J. (2014). Neuroscience reveals that boredom hurts. *Phi Delta Kappan*, *95*(8), 28–32.

Wiliam, D. (2007). Content *then* process: Teacher learning communities in the service of formative assessment. In D. Reeves (Ed.), *Ahead of the curve: The power of assessment to transform teaching and learning* (pp. 183–201). Bloomington, IN: Solution Tree Press.

Wiliam, D. (2011). *Embedded formative assessment*. Bloomington, IN: Solution Tree Press.

INDEX

Bringing Homework Into Focus
Eileen Depka

In many classrooms, teachers assign homework out of habit. Learn to design quality, purposeful homework instead. The author urges educators to reflect on the purpose of student assignments to determine if and when homework is valuable. Prepare students and measure their comprehension by assigning purposeful work, setting clear expectations, and providing feedback as the unit of study unfolds.
BKF616

The Five Dimensions of Engaged Teaching
Laura Weaver and Mark Wilding

Engaged teaching recognizes that educators need to offer more than lesson plans and assessments for students to thrive in the 21st century. Equip your students to be resilient individuals, able to communicate effectively and work with diverse people. The authors contend that students must develop their emotional and social skills as thoroughly as their academic skills, and that teachers must cultivate this growth.
BKF601

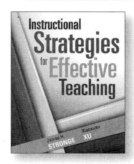

Instructional Strategies for Effective Teaching
James H. Stronge and Xianxuan Xu

Discover the keys to improving student learning and success. Taking a practical approach to instructional delivery, the authors outline research-based strategies and illustrate how teachers, coaches, and administrators can use them to enhance their everyday practices. Organized around ten methods of instruction, this user-friendly guide will help teachers dig deep into classroom discussion, concept mapping, inquiry-based learning, and more.
BKF641

Creating Purpose-Driven Learning Experiences
William M. Ferriter

Motivate and inspire students to learn at high levels. By bringing meaningful work to the classroom, students will develop curiosity, become actively engaged, and have a sense of purpose for their education. Discover strategies and tips for reshaping the traditional classroom environment to give modern students opportunities to exercise choice in their curriculum, master skills, and demonstrate what they've learned.
BKF691

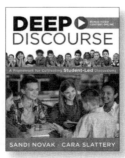

Deep Discourse
Sandi Novak and Cara Slattery

When educators provide explicit instruction, guidance, and feedback to students and let them steer the dialogue, students develop essential critical-thinking, problem-solving, and self-directed learning skills. This book details a framework for implementing student-led classroom discussions that improve student learning, motivation, and engagement across all levels and subject areas. The text features tools, tips, and exercises, plus unrehearsed videos of student-led classroom discussions.
BKF725

Solution Tree | Press

a division of

Solution Tree

Visit SolutionTree.com or call 800.733.6786 to order.

Wait! Your professional development journey doesn't have to end with the last pages of this book.

We realize improving student learning doesn't happen overnight. And your school or district shouldn't be left to puzzle out all the details of this process alone.

No matter where you are on the journey, we're committed to helping you get to the next stage.

Take advantage of everything from **custom workshops** to **keynote presentations** and **interactive web and video conferencing**. We can even help you develop an action plan tailored to fit your specific needs.

Let's get the conversation started.

Call 888.763.9045 today.

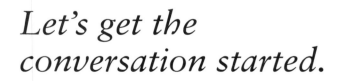

 SolutionTree.com